THE THINGS WOMEN ENDURE

Learning to Love Yourself

SHALETHA MARSHALL

The Things Women Endure : Learning to Love Yourself

Copyright © 2019 by Shaletha Marshall.

All rights reserved, including the right to reproduce this book or portions thereof in any form whatsoever. No part of this production may be reproduced or transmitted in any form or by any means, mechanical or electronic, including photocopying or recording, or by any information storage and retrieval system, or transmitted by email without permission in writing form the publisher.

Scripture quotations are taken from The New King James Version (NKJV), New Living Translation (NLT), New American Standard Bible (NASB), and King James Version (KJV) of the bible © 1973, 1978, 1980, 1982, 1984 by the International Bible Society and from www.biblegateway.com.

Published by :

Relentless Publishing House, LLC

www.relentlesspublishing.com

ISBN : 978-1948829298

First Edition : August 2019

Dedication

Zion Imani Marshall you are the love of my life and I wouldn't trade it for anything. I now know what the true meaning of Love is and blessed beyond measures that God chose me to be your mother.

I want to thank everyone who was my support system that took my calls and heard my cries throughout this rough time in my life. I love you all!

Table Of Contents

In the Beginning	7
20 and Young	9
Real Life	11
The Party Girl	13
Downhill Spiral	17
Settling Down	21
No More Us	23
The New Guy	25
Having Fun	27
Moving Out	29
Is This Love	31
Looking For a Home	33
Stripping Days	35
Sugar Daddy	37
Moving Day	39
Valet Parking	41
Living the Good Life	43
Friend Zone	45
Nathan Moves In	47
High Come Down	51
Locked Up	53
Finding the Right Girl	55
We Found One	57
God Changed Things Up	61

Meeting My Husband	65
Courtship	67
The Proposal	71
The Marriage	75
Our Wedding Day	77
Moving on with Our Lives	81
Texas Here We Come	85
Going Back to Work	87
God's Doing a New Thing	91
Jezebel Spirit	95
Who's Baby	101
This Feels Like Death	103
Broken Promises	105
Getting My Life Together	107
Meeting My Ishmael	109
What Kind of Man Are You ?	117
Seeking After God	121
The Divorce	125
About the Author	135

Love, Grace, Mercy, Peace, Increase, Joy, Trust, Promotion, Healing, Protection, Favor and Forgiveness are all promises from God that He will never forsake you.

"Therefore, having these promises, beloved, let us cleanse ourselves from all filthiness of the flesh and spirit, perfecting holiness in the fear of God." 2 Corinthians 7:1-NKJV

Father I humbly come to you today ready to receive your favor, grace and mercy over my life. I cast out all my fears unto you Lord. I cast out all my cares and worries unto you Father. I put my trust in you knowing that you will bring me to a flourishing finish. I give you all the desires in my life. Amen!

In the Beginning

When you are young, you don't think about the things that you would go through as an adult. School doesn't teach you about the real world and how mean these streets are. There are no handbooks or guidelines to follow on how to survive life beyond your front door.

As a baby, you began to learn how to comprehend living outside of your mother's womb. The brain is developing and you learn your parents' voice and eventually you began to smile at them. It becomes a routine of them smiling at you because they notice you smiling at them. The next phase is that they try to mimic you and speak. Speaking just doesn't come natural to a baby, they watch you and study your mouth movements.

I can remember when my daughter was trying to figure out what my mouth was doing as I talked to her and she would just lay there and watch my lips move. It was the funniest thing to me, and then she would begin to move her mouth but with no sound. That's how we are in real life watching, looking and studying other people; being molded into someone else's image with no sound.

Yes, you develop a routine in waking up every morning to get ready for school for twelve years, but is that really what life has to offer? We are not taught what the word says about us going through trials and tribulations. We are not taught that there will be some good days and there will be some bad days. We have to understand that there are stages in life that we must go through and realize that our life is not our own, it belongs to the Lord. God will help guide us and try to stir us into finding our purpose but without true knowledge and guidance, you will find yourself stuck or lost.

Growing up you are being shaped by who and what your parents want you to be. You are made to do house chores, but at that time you don't see it as helping you to become a responsible person. Learning to cook and clean is very beneficial for living on your own.

As a child you take for granted the rules that are put into place to help with your own personal experiences. As a teenager you are taught to be independent. You have to go to school, play a sport, work or help take care of your siblings while your parents work. You began to put God on the back burner. You don't understand the meaning of putting God first until you've experienced things in life.

"But seek first the kingdom of God and His righteousness, and all these things shall be added to you."
Matthew 6:33 -NKJV

20 and Young

I have been on my own since I was 20 years old and not one time did I ever say that I didn't want to cook or clean up after myself. I actually enjoyed doing those things. One year I was living in Statesboro, GA, with my sister, while she attended college, I ended up cooking and cleaning to get money. I was doing this for some college boys around campus who didn't know how to cook, clean or just didn't have the time.

I am thankful that I was able to learn how to cook, clean and do laundry because I didn't have to wait on someone else to do those things for me. I see parents these days asking their child to do this and do that and bribe them by saying if you clean up you will get something. I don't believe in that type of parenting style. If you have your own room or bathroom you should want to keep it clean because that's your personal space.

> *"Therefore the Lord has recompensed me according to my righteousness, According to my cleanness in His eyes."*
> *2 Samuel 22:25 -NKJV*

One client paid me weekly to do his laundry and clean up his apartment. He played football so he wasn't really at home enough to get those things done and I didn't mind because I needed the money and I liked being alone. Another client wanted me to cook and clean for him so I would go to the store and get the items I needed to make his favorite meals. And I would go over while he was at school because he left a key for me to have the food ready for when he returned home. So, I would prepare the food and clean up while the food was in the oven.

Just from those basic house rules I learned as a child I was able to use it for my benefit. I did that for about one year in order to buy the things that I wanted or needed. School doesn't teach you when you graduate from high school that bills are a life of their own. School doesn't teach you how hard life is and that you will have more bills than money in your bank account at times. That is how most people can go to college and never do anything other than stay in school, because it's hard to get a job straight out of school unless you or your family knows someone high up in a good company.

Real Life

Once you start to have children it's a whole different ball game. That's why I chose not to have kids at a young age. Don't get me wrong, I ran the streets and had a lot of male friends but I was not that interested in boys like that in school.

I can remember my mom always saying that if you have sex you would get pregnant. Since she had me at 16 years old, I thought that statement was to be true. My sisters and I would always make jokes on how we better not have sex so that we would not get pregnant.

That statement became true once I found out that I was pregnant at 19 and still living at home with my mom. I could not believe that I ended up pregnant and didn't know what to do.

I was dating a guy a couple of years older than me and I was in college, so I hid it from my mom as long as I could. I continued to go to school and work like nothing was different. And then one day out of the blue she asked the million-dollar question, "Shaletha are you pregnant?"

I was like "huh, what are you talking about," she said "I just know." I still could not bring myself to tell her the truth so I lied and said no.

It seems like immediately after she asked me about being pregnant, I started to show and began to have morning sickness. I was not ready to except the truth so I continued to hide it from everyone, even my then boyfriend.

"The discretion of man deferreth his anger; and it is his glory to pass over a transgression."
Proverbs 19:11 -KJV

I continued with my daily routine and hiding my pregnancy from the world. The morning sickness became too much for me. I was not able to eat, drink or even swallow my own saliva.

So, I ended up telling my boyfriend first that I was almost 3 months pregnant and didn't want to keep the baby. He said that he needed some time to think about it. I informed him that we needed to tell my mom and he agreed.

One night he came over to our place and we sat her down in the living room proceeding to tell her what she already knew. That was one of the scariest moments in my adult life and it was definitely a real struggle on what to do because I strongly believe in God and what He would think of me having an abortion.

John, my boyfriend at the time, wanted me to keep the baby but I did not like the way that I was feeling. I was throwing up everywhere and still could not eat anything. I finished school for that semester and took a break because I couldn't do anything but lay in bed.

I was tired of being sick so I talked it over with my mom and prayed to God that he would forgive me for what I wanted to do and made the decision to get an abortion. I found a clinic that could get me in that following week and what to expect.

I was very hurt, disappointed and more importantly I felt like God was not going to forgive me for the sin that I was about to commit. It took me a long time to forgive myself for my disobedience even though I was not ready to have a baby at 19.

"God comforts us in all our troubles so that we can comfort others. When we are weighed down with troubles, it is for your comfort and salvation! For when we ourselves are comforted, we will certainly comfort you. Then you can patiently endure the same things we suffer." 2 Corinthians 1:4-6 -NLT

"We can say with confidence and a clear conscience that we have lived with a God-given holiness and sincerity in all our dealings. We have depended on God's grace, not on our own human wisdom. That is how we have conducted ourselves before the world, and especially toward you."
2 Corinthians 1:12 –NLT

The Party Girl

As the years went on it seemed like I had problem after problem, issue after issue. Things just couldn't seem to go right in my life and I had no one to blame but myself. I starting partying, doing drugs and hanging out with the wrong people who I thought were my friends.

"Yet the body is not for immorality, but for the Lord, and the Lord is for the body. Now God has not only raised the Lord, but will also raise us up through His power. Do you not know that your bodies are members of Christ? Shall I then take away the members of Christ and make them members of a prostitute? May it never be!"
1 Corinthians 6:13-15 -NASB

While God was waiting on me, I was being put in test after test. If I knew then what I know now, I wouldn't have gone through life seeking something that I never was going to find. If I knew then what I know now I would have never given my body away to sexual sin. And if I knew then what I know now I wouldn't have gone through half of the bad things that I did.

"The presence of adolescents' fears existing simultaneously with adult ambition is not isolated to the journey of womanhood."
-Sarah Jakes Roberts

'Lord I'm nothing without you. I am covered by your grace regarding every aspects of my life. Please forgive me for all of my sins. Nothing about you is insignificant and as a child of the most high I am covered in

your love.'

Once I realized what was going on, I was twenty-one and God was right there waiting with His arms stretched out wide open. But me being young, I wasn't fully ready to submit and accept God's word. So, He continued to put me through a series of tests.

I started to go to jail, I lost jobs and my car got repossessed. I know that you can relate to some of those things happing. I guess with all the stress that I was under, I had a miscarriage without me fully understanding what was going on, or was it God paying me back for what I had done two years before?

We were at home one night watching TV like normal and then all of a sudden, my stomach began to hurt really bad and it felt like I had to use the restroom. So, I got up and went to the bathroom and a big red clump came out and I started to bleed. I thought that my cycle had started because it wouldn't stop and I bled for about two weeks after that night.

Not sure what happened between us but John began to cheat on me and ended up moving out of the apartment that I had in my name for us and took all of the furniture that my mom bought for me while I was in jail for speeding.

Once you get in the system it seems like you can go to jail for any and every little thing. And through all of that, I was still not ready to submit my life over to God. Even though I went through those life experiences, I don't regret any of it because it has made me into the women that I am today.

Downhill Spiral

We take for granted life's lessons and teachings while growing up. I was raised in church and living with my grandmother who was a minister, I went to church 3 - 4 times a week, so I knew right from wrong. But for some reason it was so easy to just do wrong.

I knew Christ was the way to go but I was letting the sinful lifestyle I chose take over my thought process. I can remember saying, "When I get grown, I am not going to church anymore," and to be honest that is exactly what I did.

When I moved to Atlanta with my mom at 18, it was very easy to get out of that habit because she didn't go to church. That made it easy for the devil to slither his way into my life, and not having that spiritual covering that my grandmother and aunt provided for me, left me wide open.

"I began to go through redemptive suffering. Redemptive suffering is when you go through a problem or pain for the benefit of others. For the weapons of our warfare are not carnal, but mighty through God to the pulling down of strong holds." 2 Corinthians 10:4 -KJV

I was young in a new city and cute. It was the start of my downfall. Partying all the time, you began to meet all types of people. I had something to do just about every night of the week not realizing that I was getting further away from God, further away from the destiny God had for my life.

I felt like it was okay since I was grown. Living with my aunt I couldn't really do much and when I did go out. I had a midnight curfew. That was not fun at all. It didn't help that I didn't have a vehicle, so I had to ride with my friends and most of the time they did not want to take me back home when we had just got to where we were going.

So, I would get locked out of the house. Once again, I do not regret anything that I did or went through early on in life because at the end of the day I know that God has always kept His loving arms around me with His angels covering me. I was 20 years old and took a road trip with my male friends to Detroit. I could remember that everything was going well, it seemed like it was going to be a great trip. We checked into our hotel and went back out so that one of the guys could go see some of his family members and then we would go eat.

I would never forget this night. This night changed my life forever and how I became street smart. We were leaving his aunt's house and one of his cousins decided that he was going to go with us. While we were sitting in our rental car waiting on him to come out, someone walked up to the vehicle with a gun and pointed it at my friend's head who was in the driver's seat. I was in the passenger seat so therefore I could see what was going on.

I thought that this was a joke by one of their friends because no one said anything but to my surprise this situation was not a joke. I guess that I was the only one who saw him, so I motioned for my friend to turn around and that's when the atmosphere in the car changed. The guy standing at the window with the gun pointed at us and said "give me all of your money and jewelry". I couldn't think, I couldn't move and I couldn't speak. Not sure how, but my friend and I jumped out of the car at the same time and took off running down the street.

I didn't know what to do or where to go, it was like every man for themselves at that moment. And then he started chasing behind us shooting. I was so scared because I had never been in that type of situation before. I didn't see anyone else so all I could do was run. You would have thought that I was in track the way that I was moving and hopping over fences. At that time, I was a buck twenty, so I was smaller than I am now and I saw this car at the back of a house and sled myself right underneath it to hide so that I wouldn't get hit by one of those bullets.

Not one time did I feel like God had left my side. I would still get intuitions on certain things or situations, so I knew that He was there. No matter what life throws at you don't forget your promised divine blessings. Ask God for wisdom, discernment and peace as you wait for Him to come through for you in your timely victory. I started back going to church but I was never active, just heard the word and went home.

And that became my routine for a while until I fell off again. I would work, hang out and then go to church on Sundays. Therefore, I was never able to meet anyone that could really help and guide me into a better understanding of God and His word.

Year after year it seemed that I was on to the next guy hanging out while having fun with no care in the world while having sex. If I only knew then, what I know now I would be a totally different person. I would have never trained myself "get you before you get me attitude." Meaning that, I would have one-night stands if I was attracted to you. I would have sex with a guy and I would get up and leave before he could have the opportunity to ask me to leave. If a guy came to my place, I would have him leave and not stay the night. That's how you really catch feelings, laying up, cuddling and having pillow talk; I didn't want to have any attachments.

But I was young and cute; I just wanted to have fun. I wanted to do things my way. I wanted to do things on my own terms without being forced to do something.

"Flee immorality. Every other sin that a man commits is outside the body, but the immoral man sins against his own body. Or do you not know that your body is a temple of the Holy Spirit who is in you, whom you have from God, and that you are not your own? For you have been bought with a price: therefore, glorify God in your body." 1 Corinthians 6:18-20 -NASB

Settling Down

I'll say around 22 I was ready to settle down. At that time my boyfriend and I got an apartment together which was exciting for me because he was a cute, sexy Jamaican. We did a lot together; he knew my family and I knew his. His sisters and I became very close. Come to find out I was the same age as one of them, so we had a lot in common.

At first it was hard to win his mom over because he was younger than me and she wanted to know what I was doing with her baby. But surprisingly he did not act his age, which he did lie to me about him being 18 years old. When his mom told me his age, I was like WTH, why am I talking to this little boy!

I have never talked to anyone younger than me, let alone someone the same age as me. I didn't know what to do because I really did like him and of course the "D" was good so what's a girl to do? Kevin said that he lied because he knew that a lady like me would not have given him the time of day who was still living at home with his mom. So, we continued to date and move in together because I was able to get past his age since his was so mature.

Living with him was actually fun and a breath of fresh air compared to living with John. There was no fighting, no arguing over little simple things and most importantly I did not have to worry about him cheating on me. We did everything together and as a family. He showed me how to cook Jamaican food and I showed him how to cook the American food he liked to eat. We even dressed alike sometimes when we stepped out. I really did enjoy being in a relationship with him and at that point age didn't matter anymore because we were together for a year and living together.

Then life changed once he meets Maurice at our job. He was two years younger than Kevin so they hit it off and started hanging out together. They started doing a lot of things together like play basketball, working out, and then it became going out to the club.

That's when things started to change because of lifting he was finally able to gained some weight and like the attention he was starting to get. Which I was cool with it because I did like the way he was looking and how his body was starting to change. I tried to hang out with them but it was not the same because I felt that Maurice was a little childish.

They continued to hang out without me and eventually Kevin began to feel like why I needed a girlfriend while all my homies were single. He wanted to be able to come and go when he wanted to and not check in, because that wasn't cool.

We ended up making it to two years with Kevin trying to balance being in a relationship and hanging out with his friends and the pressure was becoming too much for him of not being single. When I am with you, I am loyal to you and our relationship.

They would tease him about having to go home or him calling me to tell me his next move. But what people don't realize is that it's called respect not checking in. So, I thought oh this is a phase he will get tired of this life, and tired of spending a lot of money. Even though he was hanging out now that didn't stop me from doing the things that I liked to do or hang out with my girlfriends.

No More Us

Then that dreadful day came when he told me that he didn't want to be in a relationship anymore, and that he wanted to date other people. I really didn't say much because I felt it in my spirit that things were changing because we began to argue about little simple stuff.

> *"Therefore we do not lose heart, though outwardly we are wasting away, yet inwardly we are being renewed day by date. For our light and momentary troubles are achieving for us an eternal glory that far outweighs them all. So we fix our eyes not on what is seen, but on what is unseen, since what is seen is temporary, but what is unseen is eternal."*
> 2 Corinthians 4:16-18 –KJV

So, I honored his wishes but we continued to live together without being in a relationship not realizing that we would open doors to new problems in our relationship. While he continued to hang now, he started staying out all night without letting me know. And I had to get used to that, I would go out and come back home at a decent time and get mad that he wasn't respecting me anymore.

A couple of months after our breakup I found condoms in his car. In that moment, when I realized that we were not going to stay together and I needed to figure out my next move and not wait around on him. I can tell that he felt bad about me finding the condoms but I did not want to know any details so I didn't ask any questions. And that's how we continued living together, don't ask and don't tell.

I wanted to do things on my own terms without being forced to do something.

The New Guy

By this time, I was working at Verizon. I started talking with this guy who was interested in me, but I would never entertain him because I was in a relationship. Sometimes he flirted with me and I flirted back, because it was nice getting some attention.

One night I was super bored and didn't want to stay in the house another weekend, so I called Nathan to see what he was up to that night. By my surprise he answered the phone and we talked for a second and agreed to meet up.

We met somewhere close to my house and I got in the car with him. We got some food in Tucker, GA, and went to the Red Roof Inn, not because that was something that he wanted to do but because I was nervous about being seen out with another guy.

It was actually cool hanging out with him alone because I got to know him and talk about life and what was going on with each of us. I felt really comfortable around him and was able to be myself. While at work he was my supervisor, so all he knew was the young, quiet girl, Shaletha.

We hung out for the rest of the night not realizing what time it was because we were enjoying each other's company. I think it was 4 am when we left the hotel falling asleep while talking all night getting to know each other.

He had a rule that his girlfriend and him made up, that he had to be home before the sun come up. I know what you are thinking, "his girlfriend?" They had a complicated relationship, so it wasn't like I was messing up anything or him cheating.

This was the first time that I had stayed out this long so I didn't know what to expect when I got home. The good thing is that I only lived 15 minutes away from where Kevin and I lived. Now on the other hand Nathan lived 30 minutes away south.

The next day Nathan stopped by the store I was working at before his shift started, because we worked on the weekends as well and it was going to be a long day. He wanted to see me and that morning for some reason, Nathan looked really good to me, like it was my first time seeing him, plus I love a man in slacks and a collared shirt. He always made sure that his clothes were on point.

So, before that day, I never really paid any attention to him because a lot of guys at my job wanted to go out with me, but I was not interested in them like that. We all were friends and began to hang out in group settings so they were more like my homeboys than anything.

Having Fun

Nathan was different though; he had this kind of swag that really intrigued me and besides he didn't sweat me like some of the other guy's did. I do not like a thirsty man.

We would have a lot of job events and he would come in with his jeans and timberlands on looking straight up like a New Yorker, and we would hang out flirting with each other because by that time we had already started talking and texting each other on the phone.

The more and more my ex hung out, it left me available to hang out as well. Nathan and I started doing everything together and working the same hours so that we were able to get off at the same time. We would rush home change clothes and literally meet up somewhere, because he still lived at home with his girl and I lived with my ex.

I began to spend time with him and his friends and sometimes go out on double dates, we always had a good time whatever we did and they knew how to party but in a different way not like the club seen that I was used too.

They were all older than me so I had to make sure that I kept my cool at all times because I did not want to seem like this young girl, but to be honest I don't think no one knew my age.

Hanging out with them was amazing to me because they were on a different level from what I was used to seeing. They all had really good jobs or companies of their own and a part of a motorcycle club so that was definitely the icing on the cake.

When he would take me riding, I felt like I was the baddest chick in ATL and you couldn't tell me anything. They never made me feel different or that I didn't belong around them. It was such a turn on to see him riding or when I would hear his bike coming into my neighborhood. I would get so excited like a little kid with butterflies in her stomach.

It was easy with him because he lived at home with his girlfriend and I was living at home with my ex-boyfriend. Over time things changed when my ex, Kevin, wanted to start dating someone that he met. So of course, I felt some type of way because I thought that he would get over it, but he didn't.

Even though Kevin and I weren't together anymore we still got alone with each other especially in front of other people. By this time my sister was getting married and we attended the wedding together because my family knew of him and of course we made a cute couple for pictures.

Two months after that was my graduation from college and I didn't think much of it because of my living situation but Kevin really came through for me and planned out the night for me with my friends and family at a restaurant and a bouquet of flowers. It was so nice to be together like that because we hadn't spent time with each other in months.

Moving Out

One day my friend and I were talking and I was telling him about my living situation and how I was ready to leave but didn't have anywhere to go, he mentioned that he knew someone that owned townhomes in Smyrna, Ga and was looking to get the rest of the building rented out and could get me into a spot.

In two weeks, he hit me up to let me know that I could move into a two-bedroom townhome that following week and I knew then that was the route that God wanted me to go. I was a little nervous because I have never lived by myself and wasn't sure on what all to do, so I called my mom and she made all the arrangements for me to move out.

We live in a one-bedroom apartment, so it wasn't much stuff to pack up, so while the movers were moving things, we were packing up my things. I felt that it was best to get moved out before Kevin got home because I don't do well with goodbyes.

I went from living in Norcross for 2 ½ years with Kevin to living 30 minutes away in Smyrna from all of my friends and family and it took a while to get used to but Nathan was there every step of the way. He helped me unpack, get food, and cable for the place. I guess he figured since he would be coming over let me help her get situated.

> *"But thanks be to God, which giveth us victory through our Lord Jesus Christ."*
> **1 Corinthians 15:57 –KJV**

It was very different living on that side of town. I knew how to get around from every store and from where I got my car maintenance, not to mention that my mom only lived 15 minutes away from me so it was really easy for her to come and help me pack up.

She got to my place with a U-Haul and two guys that were great at moving. Where I lived it was easy to find people who wanted to work and make some cash, so they had me all packed up and ready to go in no time.

I had to learn how to cook for one person which was really hard for me because I've never lived alone before and I genuinely enjoyed cooking for other people. So that was something new for me, even when I lived with my sister, I cooked all the time while she baked desserts. That was just something that we liked to do

Is This Love?

Wikipedia defines love as a variety of strong and positive emotional and mental states, ranging from the most sublime virtue or good habit, the deepest interpersonal affection and to the simplest pleasure.

By this time, I had been living by myself for a month now and I was pretty much seeing Nathan every day. If you saw him you saw me right there with him. I knew all of his friends and he knew all of mine and that is what helped me become comfortable with living on my own. There was no one checking on my coming and going or who I was talking to and it felt great.

As the months went on everything was really good with Nathan but I started to develop more intimate feelings for him and I didn't like that he was still going home to his ex-girl, and at first I understood because they had just bought a house one year before meeting me so it was convenient for him to stay there and now one year later he was leaving me some nights to go home.

Maybe I was naive for believing what he was telling me but our situation ship was easy. We spent just about every day together so how could I not begin to fall in love with him. Some days we even worked together because he switched his schedule based off of mine.

So therefore, I knew that he was not dealing with his ex-anymore. On the nights that we were not together we would talk on the phone for hours because he was living in another room as if they were roommates.

I knew everything about her and her daughter so he was definitely there for convenience because he put all his money into the house thinking that they were going to get married, I guess that she wanted to know about me because she began to call me but would never say anything and I knew that it was her because she would call every time he was on his way to my place.

Two years into our relationship I wanted more from him, he my family and I knew his family as well. I was definitely not the side chick because we were going out of town every three months spending time with his family and just us getting away for the week.

I was beginning to get confused on us because I didn't understand how we were doing all these things together but he would not move out and get his own place. He never made me feel insecure or that I couldn't trust him, I just wanted him all to myself.

Looking for A Home

It was two and a half years later that I gave him an ultimatum of moving out or we would not see each other anymore because I was totally invested in him and knew that I wanted more. Even though he would spend nights it just wasn't enough.

My lease on the townhome was coming to an end and I wanted to purchase a home for myself so that I would not have to depend on anyone anymore. So, I began to make preparations for that and once again Nathan was right there beside me every step of the way. I took up a second job part time as a cashier in 2005 for a valet parking company and took a break from school so that I could focus on work and saving money.

The process started off rocky because my credit was bad which was weird because I hadn't had anything in my name since my first car and apartment. Come to find out my mom had been using my credit since I was in high school.

I began to read up on the laws and spoke to the creditors and informed them that the things that were on my credit were not from me and that I was in high school with most of the things on there.

So, I had to provide them with a copy of my ID and my high school transcript with a letter stating why I was disputing the items and by God's favor everything was removed and my credit went up within 60 days. I was super excited because now I had a better chance of getting something new to my liking.

Once I started back looking at houses, I ended up finding the perfect starter home and it was in my price range. Now this home was in

McDonough, Ga way on the other side of town from my job, family, and friends. But I didn't care because it was a perfect two-story home with an all-white kitchen and most importantly it was going to be all mine with no one's help except from God of course. We put the offer in two days later so that the seller could take it off the market. I really did want the house and loved everything about it, I just felt so comfortable in the house and I knew that is where God wanted me to be.

Now that I think about, God was putting me in isolation and setting me up to be with Him and focus on Him more. But I didn't see that, I didn't realize that He wanted more of me and more of my time. Even though He was blessing me with everything I wanted I didn't give God more of my time.

Then the issues started to come. The seller didn't want to pay closing, didn't want to pay to get the paint touched up and didn't want to clean up the home before I moved in. He figured that since he didn't live there he didn't need to, but at the end of the day it was his responsibility to get those things done if he wanted the house sold. So, he did curve on some things and paid to get the house paint touched up, and get cleaned but we had to find the companies. Thankfully my realtor knew people and was able to find someone to clean and paint the house within the budget that the seller gave.

I was beyond excited about getting this house I felt that I was so deserving of it because of all the things that I had been through and to not depend on anyone else getting me a place or putting me out of a place was such a blessing to me. Not that I had a hard life, I just made some poor choices.

I wasn't working a steady job because going to jail five times within the last three years made it impossible to keep a job. So, I had to do other things in order to make money so that I could pay my bills and my probation fine. I ended up becoming an exotic dancer for this group of guys that had a couple of girls working for them.

Stripping Days

To be honest I was super nervous and didn't know what to do so I watched some videos on how to move and dance. I didn't have any clothes for that so I just wore a bathing suit and high heels until I had extra money to get some appropriate clothes.

The guy's never put us in an uncomfortable situation and they always stayed with us to make sure nothing crazy happened. They pretty much did everything for us, including getting all of our appointments set up so it was easy money. I never did anything that I didn't want to do and no one ever forced me to drink or do drugs, so I was very aware of what was going on at every party.

That became my life for a couple of years and my family didn't know anything and I wanted to keep it that way because I felt a little embarrassed about having to go that route in order to get money to pay bills.

After that first year of doing parties, I moved into the clubs because I needed more money to pay off my probation fine. I felt that was keeping me locked down of not being able to get a job. The strip club was very different from doing small parties. I had to basically interview to work inside of a strip club and the girls were not friendly at all when someone new started. I didn't let that stop me. I had a plan and needed to stick with that plan. I was very focused on what I had to do and didn't let that life consume me. I worked my shift and left. I didn't make any friends nor did I hang out where I worked.

"No one can serve two masters. For you will hate one and love the other, you will be devoted to one and despise the other. You cannot serve both God and money."
Matthew 6:24 -KJV

Sugar Daddy

One night I meet this Jamaican truck driver who lived in Ga but on the road most of the time. He would come into the club for drinks when he was in town. We started talking and he paid me to just sit and talk with him, so I looked forward to those nights.

I didn't like being in that place but I had to for the time being so it was nice to have someone see me for me and not just a sex object. We became close and one day he was telling me how he didn't like that I was working there and ask me what I was doing there. So, I explained to him my situation and he made me an offer to stop working there and he would take care of my bills.

At that time, I was 22 years old and that sounded really good because I didn't like stripping anyway. So, I thought about it and wanted to make sure that he was for real because stuff like this just doesn't happen in real life. I continue working there because I didn't believe him and wondered why he would do this for me.

The next time he came into the club and saw me he was very mad that I was there and asked me to leave and he would give me the money that I would have missed out on. So, we met up and talked about what he wanted from me and it was very simple. He basically wanted some arm candy when he was in town, sounds like a great plan to me.

When he would come into town, he would call me and I would meet up with him for dinner or at sports bars pretty much wherever he wanted to go, but I always drove myself. I never rode in cars with guys ever since that one night I was robbed at gunpoint and shot at while visiting Michigan.

I wanted to have control over my life as much as I could. And he made good on his word. He started giving me money, buying groceries for my sister and I and all I had to do was answer his call. This was the best setup that I've ever encountered. So, I took advantage of the situation and focused on school so that I could finish my degree. Not having to work different shifts at the club gave me more time so therefore I was able to focus on school.

That arrangement lasted for about 8 months and it was cool, I was going out meeting people and eating good. He even took me on a couple of trips and then things changed when he told me that he wanted to have sex with me.

I should have known better because nothing in life is free, but he made it so convenient and easy. He never bothered me and I didn't bother him either and plus he had a wife and family so I wasn't trying to cause any trouble. I told him that was not something that I was comfortable doing and plus he was an older gentleman and not my type.

So he continued hanging out with me like we had before but I guess his urges were beginning to get stronger because I continued to press me, telling me that him and his wife were not having sex anymore and it had been a minute for him but I was thinking that was not my problem and I was not a hooker. So, I told him that maybe we should end our arrangement for him to find someone who wouldn't mind hanging out and having sex with him.

After that situation I just wanted to work and make my own money so I began working at Best Buy where I meet Kevin. Things were going well I was working, paying my bills and started back going to school trying to finish because I didn't go back after I had the abortion.

Not to mention I was off of probation so that was such a huge weight lifted off of me. No more talking to men for money. No more getting into trouble with the law. And most importantly no more looking over my shoulders. I was so grateful for working and being able to purchase my own house.

Moving Day

I cannot believe it, today is the day that I actually move into my new home. No more looking for a place to live. No more asking someone to help me out. And by God's grace no more depending on someone to provide me with a place to live.

The manager of the parking company I was working at asked a couple of guys to help me move from Smyrna to McDonough in just a couple of hours. I was so grateful for their help because I didn't know how I was going to move myself, everyone that I knew was at work and I didn't want to wait. They were able to get most of the big stuff put together and whatever they didn't get to Nathan came over to help me once he got off work.

> *"Be merciful to me, O Lord for I am calling on you constantly. Give me happiness O Lord, for I give myself to you. O Lord, you are so good, so ready to forgive, so full of unfailing love for all who ask for your help."*
> **Psalms 86:3-5 -NLT**

I was really falling in love with him and knew that he loved me too, but he just would not move out from his house or give me a real commitment. So, I started to pull away, hanging out more with my friends and spending nights out because McDonough was 40 minutes away from downtown Atlanta and where most of my friends lived.

A short while after I moved into my house I stopped working for Verizon and went full time with the valet parking company because I could make more money there. Once I became full-time, they were able to see my work ethic and offered me an assistant manager position. I like to drive but I was nervous about driving someone's car.

Valet Parking

This was definitely going to be something new for me because one, I've never driven cars like that and two, I was going to be driving someone else's car so I was anxiously nervous and three, I was going to be working with all guys. So, I am not sure how this is going to go over, but the managers assured me that I would not have any issue and the team would respect me as a female.

Since I was new to valet parking, they started me off checking in the car of the hotel guest. This didn't require me to move cars only to keep up with their keys. And I was super relieved about that. Since I had become a full-time assistant valet parking manager, I didn't have the free time that I once did, so Nathan got put on the back burner. At first, I pretty much had to work all night shifts, which was cool because I made a lot of money that way. Sometimes guests would ask me where could they get some weed from. So, I ran this idea by Nathan about him allowing me to keep some on hand so that I could get the money right then. But he wasn't having that, he thought that it would be best if I took the orders and called him to let him know what the deal was and he would come up there.

I had the advantage of working all the event parking and since I was new all the guys wanted to check in their car with me, so I was able to sell weed without having to distribute anything. That's how I was able to save up money to buy new furniture for my new house. Customers were tipping me when they checked in their car. Nathan was giving me half of the money that was being made and I was getting tipped when guest came to pick up their car. Once the guys on my shift noticed that I was getting tips and not them some wanted to work with me all the time.

So, I began to build relationships that way. Every sport, musical, or downtown event, I was there checking in cars because we worked at one of the largest hotels in downtown Atlanta. I began working 7 days a week 16 hours a day. Valet parking became my life and I loved it. I started trying to recruit other girls to work there so that I would have some friends.

I became so popular at valet that everyone wanted to park with the new pretty girl, even celebrities became some of my regular customers. This was easy work but long hours, it was definitely better than me stripping at clubs. During this season of my life, I was 25 years old and everything was going well. I was in a different place in my life and finally felt like I had a purpose and belonged to something.

I am a very fast learner so they were able to see my work ethic and the way that I could learn something and turn it around to something better. Before I knew it, I was moving up in the company and taking on different roles.

Living the Good Life

Two months after I became the valet manager, I was able to buy furniture for my house with cash. I knew how important your credit is so I didn't want to start messing it up now by putting unnecessary stuff on it.

I began to save all of my tip money so that I could buy whatever I wanted without having to get my credit ran. It was nothing for me to work long hours because I didn't have any other obligations. And some nights the guys, Sara, and I would go out somewhere especially if we had a good night in tips. We began to party all the time drinking and popping pills.

That became my new normal when I couldn't hang out with Nathan I started to pull back and started going out on dates trying to see if there were someone else out there for me. He started to suspect something was different with me and began to ask me all types of questions. I really did love and want to be with him but he just was not ready for that commitment even after 3 ½ years in. I got to the point where I was like I am going to do me and have fun and he did not like that.

About four months of me hanging out and going out on dates he tells me that he is going to move out from his house. I have never been happy to hear those words, and then I thought that maybe he was playing me telling something that I wanted to hear just to get me to stop going out and hounding him about it. In or to prepare myself for him to move in with me I decided to let all of my male friends go. Because once he moved in none of that was going to happen.

"We must break the habit of using other people as a narcotic to numb the dull aching of our inner void." - **Bishop T.D. Jakes**

Friend Zone

I felt really bad that I wasn't going to be Roberts's friend anymore. He was truly my best friend and a really good guy. He took very good care of me like he was my big brother. Whenever I needed something, he was there to make sure that I had it. It was very different than how it was with Nathan because it was not sexual or he didn't use me for things like other men had during my previous years. I trusted Robert so much that he even had a key to my house.

There were times where we would get dressed up and go out especially the times when Nathan couldn't take me out. I could tell that Robert didn't like me talking to him but hey what could he say I was in love with him. We would take turns cooking for each other and going grocery shopping for each other's place. Now Robert was fine, he was tall with a football player build, light skinned, light eyes, and good wavy hair.

He was definitely cute and could pull any girl he wanted, just not me. He was very close to my mom and her husband so we would always be around each other and I knew that it bothered him whenever Nathan would come around. We knew everything about each other and I guess that is my fault because I'm like an open book to my friends and he could not figure out how he ended up in the friend zone.

One day my mom was telling me all the things that Robert would tell her about me but what puzzled me was that he never expressed his feelings to me so I didn't know. I thought that he liked our relationship the way it was. Because we would hang out and spend the night with each other with no feelings or emotions.

When I told Robert that Nathan was moving in, I could tell that he was crushed but there was absolutely nothing that I could do because I didn't see him in that manner and I wanted to be with Nathan. I had been waiting years for this to happen. At of all the guys I've dating this is the only one that I was truly in love with and wanted to be a family with.

Nathan Moves In

Seems like it took forever for Friday to get here and for Nathan to get off work. By this time, I was working 6am - 2pm and was already home showered, dressed and had dinner cooked. I was beyond excited and didn't know what to expect because I hadn't lived with a guy since 2003.

He pulled up to my house around 6pm with all of his clothes, but not everything. I didn't let that bother me because he was there and finally giving me what I wanted. I was excited like I had just found out that I was pregnant.

At this moment and time there was no more of my hanging out with male friends. No more having random sex and no more doing drugs. I was devoted to him and making sure that I could be the best girlfriend that he could ever have.

I switched my off days to what his were so that we could have more time to hang out with each other besides on the weekends. We would go to different places and site see, buy random things, go eat at different restaurants or just whatever life presented us that day.

Our off days were on a Monday so he ended up calling it, "Money Mondays," because we would try to do everything on that one day since that was or only off day. Quality time is my love language so most of the time we wouldn't do anything specific just walk around. As long as he was with me and gave me his full attention, I was good. He didn't need to buy me anything and we didn't need to get all dressed up. I loved him for who he was.

We had been talking about bringing another girl into the mix for a couple of months now and I had finally agreed to it since we were living together. I had wanted to experience that feeling again since the last time it happened when I was 21 years old and my female friend was older than me.

My friend and I hung out all the time clubbing and going to parties together, so when that happened it kind of caught me off guard. We never talked about those types of things; she never mentioned to me that she was like that or even interested in me.

One night we were hanging out like we always did after the club and we stopped by her friend's house to smoke. Before we got there, we stopped to get some food because we definitely would want to eat afterwards. The three of us would always drink, eat, and just chill out.

That particular night I fell asleep on the couch and woke up to her sucking on my breast. I was in complete shock as to what was happening to me that I was not able to speak. But at the same time, it was feeling so good. I thought to myself, "Lord, what is happening with me?" Then she proceeded to go down on me and then my flesh took over because it was a feeling that I had never felt before. How do I tell her to stop when I was coming to my eruptive point? How do I say to my best friend, "What the hell are you doing?" when I was on a totally different kind of high? All I could do was to embrace it.

I was quiet the entire ride back to my house. She didn't say anything and neither did I. A week went by and I didn't hear from her. I called her to see what was up and to hang out like we normally did and to find out was that a one-time thing or was that something she wanted to do again because I did. She didn't answer. Another week went by and this time she called me to go out to this party. Same as all the other times, she came to pick me up and we hung out drinking, dancing with each other. This time I was nervous because I did not know what her thoughts were on the situation.

After the party we stopped to get something to eat because we were going to her friend's house to smoke. We got there and started to drink some more and dancing to the music that he was playing while we waited on him to finish rolling up. This time she started to kiss me and I couldn't believe that I was actually enjoying kissing another woman.

By this time, her male friend was sitting by her touching all over her and maybe that was the plan for him to join in but I wasn't having that and not comfortable being with another girl's man. They both understood and agreed that it was just going to be her and I while he watched. To be honest I was so high that I didn't remember that he was there. All I knew was that I wanted to feel her again.

High Come Down

The next day I got up to get ready for work and realized that I didn't have time to fix me anything to eat so I called in an order to pick up on my way to work which was close to my house. Still taking in the events from what happened the night before, I was in my own little world. As I was leaving the food place, this lady hits my car right there in the parking spot. I really don't understand how she hit the car when I wasn't even moving yet. We got out exchanging insurance information and she apologized to me and we began to go our separate ways.

Neither one of us saw her friend on the phone with the police so as I make it out of the shopping plaza a police officer pulls me over. Since I didn't do anything wrong, I pull over to see what was going on thinking that he just wanted to make sure that I was ok.

Clearly that was not his intention. He proceeds to yell, telling me to get out of the car. I'm trying to ask him why and what did I do wrong? I know my rights, but I guess that you have none once you are in the system.

I got out of the car trying to give him my ID and insurance card and he immediately began putting handcuffs on me and searched my car. By this time, I hear the lady that hit me in the background yelling "What are you doing, she didn't do anything wrong. I hit her car and I take full responsibility for what happened. Let her go!" That was my first time ever experiencing a racist police officer.

I felt humiliated, so low and so helpless at that point but I stayed calm because I knew that I was not going to win that battle. Especially since I heard him tell her to get back in her car and that the situation did not concern her.

"Injustice anywhere is a threat to justice everywhere. Darkness cannot drive out darkness; only light can do that. Hate cannot drive out hate; only love can do that. Free at last, Free at last, Thank God almighty we are free at last. In the end, we will remember not the words of our enemies, but the silence of our friends. The time is always right to do what is right. Freedom is never voluntarily given by the oppressor; it must be demanded by the oppressed. I have decided to stick with love. Hate is too great a burden to bear. The function of education is to teach one to think intensively and to think critically. Intelligence plus character - that is the goal of true education. Life's most persistent and urgent question is, 'What are you doing for others? I look to a day when people will not be judged by the color of their skin, but by the content of their character."

– Dr. Martin Luther King Jr.

Locked Up

I was in jail three months for probation violation, fleeing the scene of an accident and resisting arrest. I couldn't believe what I was hearing. I couldn't believe what was happening to me. Surely this was a dream.

At the time I was living with my sister so I called her and I was finally able to get in touch with her later that day so that she could let my manager know that I was not going to be able to make it in since we worked at the same place.

My manager was very understanding about what happened and the situation at hand. She allowed me to have off but once my sister told her that I was sentenced to three months, she informed her that she couldn't keep my job for that long. I was okay with that because she had already done more than enough by paying me for two weeks. That allowed me to have some money put on my books.

I felt like God was punishing me for the sinful acts that I was partaking in and the fact that I enjoyed it knowing that it was wrong and not God like. I started to repent, read the bible and go to bible study once a week while I was in jail. While attending I would ask God to forgive me for all of the wrongful thoughts and sins that I had and committed.

It must have worked because one Saturday afternoon I was called to go to court which is unusual because judges did not work on the weekends. I was really nervous because I was the only person there and the judge looked over my case file and said "Lynn, time served, and you are free to go home."

Now tell me that God isn't good, it was like the judge was there only for me. I was super excited and thanking God at the same time because He heard my cries and answered my prayers. I was beyond grateful for what just happened and how fast it happened. Just like that I was out of jail within three months.

Since it was so unexpected, my sister was not at home to pick me up because her boyfriend had taken her out of town for the weekend. I couldn't call her with the good news. Minutes and hours went by as I sat in the lobby waiting because I was not going to be caught walking down the highway. I was able to get in touch with my guy friend after setting up there for three hours trying not to get discouraged. Once he answered the phone I quickly yelled in the phone "can you come pick me up because no one was at home and I didn't know anyone else's phone number!"

Cain showed up in about thirty minutes which seemed like forever. He had just got home from work when I called and wanted to get cleaned up. I really didn't care anymore because I was grateful that someone finally answered the phone and was able to come and get me.

When I was able to get my car out of the pound, it was such a mess. The police had taken everything apart like I was a drug trafficker. The food that I had bought was still in the car which smelled really bad. The piece of paper which had the lady's car insurance information on it was gone from my car. I couldn't believe that a police officer would do something like that. I had to ride around with a ding on the left side bumper all because of a trifling racist cop.

I called my best friend to let her know what happened because I'm sure that she tried to reach out to me within those three months I was in jail, but there was no answer. I figured that she may be working so I waited a couple of days and called her back and still no answer. I figured that God was trying to close that chapter in my life, so I didn't reach out to her anymore. Plus, God had just got me out of jail. By no means did I want to disappoint Him.

Finding the Right Girl

Here we are, five years later, Nathan was finally living in his own apartment close to downtown Atlanta. It was really convenient for me to stay over there. Once he was all settled in, I began looking for girls online because neither one of us knew how to approach a woman off the street. It was actually easy for me to do it that way because it was less conversations and interactions with females I wasn't interested in.

Whenever we found someone that we both liked, we would set up a meet and greet with her and myself only, to see if we click. This went on for a couple of years until he found someone at the mall where they both worked.

Nathan was really excited about me meeting Judy. Initially we started talking on the phone until we agreed to meet up in person. I think she was nervous because we would talk all the time and she would see him at work once a week so it was no pressure from us. A couple of weeks later she called and agreed to meet me one Friday night at L Lounge. Then I became nervous because it took her awhile to finally make a decision so I figured that she really didn't want to.

Once we were at the restaurant we were able to talk and that's when she let me know that she didn't want to meet both of us together and I informed her that we would never do that. We wanted to make sure that the person would be comfortable with me first and then the three of us would hang out. We continued talking, drinking just enjoying the atmosphere and we hit it off really good. Come to find out she was older than me and it was going to be her first time if she decided to go along with it.

She was a cute little chocolate lady, very well put together and I was attracted to her which was weird because I normally liked light skinned girls just like my men. But I was definitely willing to give her a chance. After dinner she asked me what I was about to do and I told her that I was going back to Nathan's place because that's where I stayed at most of the time when I was working downtown. He only lived ten minutes from my job.

What Judy said next caught me completely off guard, she asked would it be okay if she came with me just to see how we all interacted with each other. So I said hold please let me call him to check and see what he is doing or if he is even at home. As I am speaking with him he is in shock of what I was telling him. This threw him for a loop because normally I would go out with girls and come back home and tell him about my date. So after fifty questions he said "okay, I guess".

We Found the One

Judy followed me to Nathan's apartment and I could tell that she was nervous and didn't know what to expect. But we are a very cool couple and can get along with anyone.

Nathan was watching the basketball game when we came in so that was the ice breaker for her to start talking to him. I went down stairs and made us something to drink because I was still nervous about her asking to come over. It normally took the other girls a couple of weeks to meet him or say no they are not interested in that or just wanted to hang out with me only.

The three of us seemed to be getting along pretty well. Laughing, talking, watching the game and drinking. When the game went off, she left. That was different and refreshing at the same time because I am used to girls being aggressive with me and it was not like that with her. We were excited about how the night went and that turned us both on to know that we may have just found the one. She was everything that we were looking for. We continued to talk on the phone until she was ready to hang out again. We didn't want to come off too strong or eager. Nathan only talked to her in passing at work since he only worked there once a week.

We became really good friends and just did girl stuff before anything sexual ever happened. I wanted to make sure that she was ready for that because once it happens there was no turning back. One night while chilling at my house the three of us were drinking and watching the game and Nathan rolled up. We began to smoke like we normally did and this time she asked if she could join in. Sure, why not, and about thirty minutes later one thing lead to another and that's how 'my girl got a girlfriend' came about.

After that night, Nathan and I agreed that we didn't want to talk to any other girls because we both enjoyed Judy's company. Once I like you, I'm down for you until you prove me otherwise. Judy and I continued to hang out and go out on dates. Things became so exclusive with us that we began spending holidays together as a three-person couple. We were in our own little bubble and our families didn't know anything about it and that is what made it even more exciting.

This three-person relationship went on for about a year, mostly with just her and I kicking it with each other until Christmas 2008. Everything was going well. I went to work and Nathan did what he normally does on Christmas Eve. When I got off work, I went to her house to help her cook our holiday dinner. We did what all girls do on holidays, cooking, singing, dancing and drinking just having ourselves a good ole time.

I ended up falling asleep at her place. When I woke up it was like 4 AM. I got up and packed up the food and made that far drive home so that I could properly get some rest and finish what I needed to cook and clean before they came over. My family was busy doing their on thang out of town so I wasn't worried about anyone coming over. Nathan got to my place around 8 AM and got in the bed with me. He had a key, therefore, he could come and go as he pleased. I was still sleepy from the previous day being at work and then going to Judy's house afterwards and I was a little tired.

A couple of hours later we got up and gathered ourselves before she got there. The plan was for her to stay the night so that we could spend all Christmas day together. Everything was going great until we exchanged our gifts. She got Nathan this nice white leather jacket and some Victoria Secrets for me. When she opened her gift from us, she was not too happy. I am not sure what the problem was or what she expected because we never discussed a budget, a wish list or who was to get what. Now mind you I buy good gifts so I couldn't figure out what the problem was until after the fact.

She expected Nathan to get us the same type of gift which I didn't know why she thought that when it was never discussed. I had gotten her bath and body works and some shirts from Charlotte Russe, which was the happening store back then. She was very quiet after the gift exchange and then decided to go home.

God Changed Things Up

I was very disappointed at how things ended for us. I really did enjoy her company and liked how we all got along together. I took it pretty hard but Nathan was like "oh well, if she wants to be petty then let her ass go. We can find someone else." I didn't want anyone else, I wanted her. I was used to her. I was comfortable with her. What could I do? She wasn't talking to us anymore, therefore, life goes on. Nathan was back online looking for us a girlfriend but everyone that he found I was not interested in. I wasn't interested in meeting someone new.

"Father in heaven, Thank you for Your faithfulness. Only you alone can satisfy me. Search my heart and remove any doubt, any uncertainty and anything that is not like you that would hold me back from what you have in store for me."

I figured that was God's way of telling me to stop living that kind of lifestyle so I started back going to church and realizing that I needed to give up Nathan as well. But I was determined to make it work because I really did love him and I knew that he loved me. I was hoping that God would change us both. We continued with our relationship the way it was and it seemed like the more I got into church and praying, the more problems we started to have. Once he moved into his condo downtown Atlanta in 2009, he began to change.

There was no more coming and going like I used to because he didn't give me a key to his new place. I had to call him every time to get through the gate inside of his area. If we were having an argument, it was nothing for him to not let me in. The condo was literally five minutes from my job so I preferred to stay over there and not have to drive 40 minutes down south to my house.

There was no doubt that he was changing or maybe it was God changing the dynamics of our relationship. I couldn't leave my clothes or a toothbrush over to his place anymore. I had to keep an overnight bag in my car. Initially I thought okay after five and a half years of us being together and doing everything together that he may be bored. I started back looking for girls online thinking that is what he wanted and hopefully that would make him go back to the way he was all of those years ago.

This time around finding girls became a real struggle because they were only interested in me. Come to find out he had his own account looking for girls and I was not too happy about that. It made me look at him differently now. One because he didn't tell me and we used to tell each other everything. And two because he was having his own conversations with girls. I don't think that he was physically cheating on me but I do think that he was flirting with other women on the dating site.

The next couple of months our relationship began to spill out of control. He had become distant and hanging out with his friends without me. I started to hang out with my friends. When he would come over, he would lock his phone or turn it off. This is a dead indication of him having something to hide. I was always able to check his phone before then, that's how I saw that he had an online dating account set up. I confronted him about having his phone locked and he stated that he locks it at work because it just be lying around. Umm yeah okay whatever you say, I'll let you think that I believe you for now. Something just wasn't sitting right in my spirit anymore and I knew that things had to change.

Of course, as a human, my flesh got in the way and I continued to have a sexual relationship with him knowing that it needed to end. I was so torn because I felt like I grew up with him. I met him when I was 22 and that time, I was 28 looking for more and he didn't want to give me more of a commitment. I continued to pray and ask God on what to do and if it was His will for us to part ways then He would have to remove Nathan out of my life.

I am not good with breaking up with someone especially him because I thought that we would be together forever. I was his best friend and he was mine. NOT! God had other plans. One day something told me to check his e-mails and I saw an e-mail from this woman stating that she had fun hanging out with him the weekend before. I e-mailed her back asking questions because I knew that if I asked him he would lie about it.

Ladies, be careful of what you wish for and take heed to your intuition. More than likely it's always right. God gave us the gift of discernment and we need to really tap into it, you can save yourself a lot of heart aches. Lord knows that I wish I did.

Even though I was hurt by his actions and he did lie, I knew that it was necessary for this to happen or else I would have stayed with him, and our time together was coming to an end. When we broke up, I didn't cry and I wasn't sad. I was at peace with it because I knew that God had worked it out for my good.

"I focus on this one thing; forgetting the past and looking forward to what lies ahead."
Philippians 3:13 -NLT

Meeting My Husband

Here it is New Year's Eve and I'm home sleep after watch night service thinking about Nathan because we would always meet up when I got out of church. But I knew that I had to stay firm on my decision of not talking to him if I wanted God to do something different with me in this new year.

While watching TV, an eHarmony commercial came on for a free week of online dating service from January 1st - January 7th, 2010. I was like okay I can try this. What's the harm and no one will ever find out that I was online looking for guys. On the 1st, I began to set up an account and began getting hits instantly. I remember thinking 'wow this is crazy I haven't even finished setting up my profile and already receiving messages from different type of guys.' I took my picture down for a minute until I was able to finish my profile. By the end of the free week I had narrowed it down to three guys that I would continue to talk to outside of the site.

The first guy I went out with was everything that I wanted on paper. He was older, had his own place and had a really good job, but what he was looking for I wasn't it. He wanted to have kids and a stay at home wife. That wasn't me, I like to work, I like to come and go when I please and I don't like checking in. We didn't talk anymore after that one night.

The second guy was okay. He was a little younger than me and had kids. He was just now getting himself together and I didn't see us working out because I was already established with my job, money, car and I had my own house so I didn't want to just settle and date someone that had kids.

The third guy was Damon. He was cool but had kids also. We started off emailing each other for the first couple of weeks. We had been talking on the phone for a while now and after the first two dates I had previously, I wasn't ready to go out with anyone else anytime soon. And plus, I was missing Nathan, so I ended up seeing him for my birthday because holidays are really important to me and he remembered to call me so we talked and I told him about my birthday party.

After a couple of days had past, I called Damon and he said, "What have you been up to and where have you been?" I lied and told him that I had been busy working and he remembered that it was my birthday a couple of days ago and he asked me what did I do. I explained to him that I had a small birthday party and he asked why he wasn't invited and to be honest I wasn't sure if Nathan was going to show so I didn't want any issues.

Courtship

I felt really bad on how I treated Damon, so I agreed that we could finally meet up. When that night came, I was tired from work and it was cold, raining outside and I just wanted to chill in the house. Damon was so persistent and really wanted to see me because we had been talking and emailing each other for almost a month now. He decided that he would drive up 40 minutes to where I lived and we would go get some movies and food to take back to my place. I was like okay that works for me because I wouldn't have to do all that driving in the rain.

Two hours later Damon was at my front door with some flowers. That was very thoughtful and sweet of him. He said that he wanted to get me something since he missed my birthday. Damon wasn't my type of dude but he was dressed nice and he did have a nice build. He was 6'1 and muscular with a thick neck, so I could rock with that for now.

We went to go grab something to eat and stopped by red box for some movies. I'm not a movie junkie so I let him pick the movies. When we got back to my place we talked, ate our food and everything was actually going well. About thirty minutes into the movie I fell asleep because it had been a long day for me. When I woke up from my nap I told him that I was sorry for falling asleep on him and said that I was going to bed because I'm not comfortable sleeping on the couch.

He seemed like a good guy so I asked him if he wanted to stay over so that he wouldn't have to drive home at 2 am. Of course, he was cool with it and I informed him that he would have to sleep on top of the covers because I wasn't ready to be intimate with anyone just yet. And like the average guy he said okay. After that night he came back over every day.

We ended up dating on and off for about 7 months. He met my family and friends and everyone was confused and wanted to know where he came from because I didn't tell anyone that I was looking and how we met. I met his family around three months of us dating. And they seemed to really like me. His kids and grandparents lived 2 ½ hours away so it would be an all-day trip.

Around August 2010 he moved in so that we could start saving money because we had been talking about marriage in the near future. He was driving 40 minutes to work and back every day until he was able to get transferred to an AT&T store close to Atlanta.

We had to get used to living with each other which was different. I like to spend time with the person I'm dating when I am not working and he likes to play video games when he wasn't working. And that would bother me because he would play for hours at a time. Now, I truly understand what being unequally yoked means and that God gives us free will to make or own decisions.

> ***"Do not be yoked together with unbelievers. For what do righteousness and wickedness have in common? Or what fellowship can light have with darkness?"***
> **2 Corinthians 6:14 -NIV**

I began to realize that I had lowered my standards and was settling. Even though he worked and had a job and car, I didn't date guys with kids. It seemed like every guy I was meeting had kids except Nathan. But I knew that I couldn't go backwards since God delivered me from that relationship with Nathan.

I should have taken that time to really focus on God. He was waiting on me to have a deeper relationship with him. Instead of praying for a guy that would love me I should have been enjoying the love that I received from God. To be honest, no one has really satisfied me the way that God has. The longing that I felt was for God all along and not man. But I didn't want to be alone and wait on God to send me the man that He designed just for me.

"O God, You are my God; I shall seek You earnestly; My soul thirsts for You, my flesh yearns for You, In a dry and weary land where there is no water."

Psalm 63:1-NASB

The Proposal

Two months later he planned this amazing day for us to hang out. I really didn't think anything of it because we were always going somewhere or on dates. But this particular day he was acting a little different; very anxious. I had some things to do, so we planned to meet back at the house around 12pm so that we could get into one car and ride together.

When I tell you, he had everything planned out, it was the best day of my life. Damon had me to pack a little bag the night before so he had everything in the car waiting on me to get home. I got home and got into his car and he had a card waiting on the seat for me to open. It was handwritten words of how much he loved me.

Our first stop was this fancy spa in Buckhead to get couple massages. It was very excellent and relaxing. That was my first time getting one with another person. After that, I was really excited because when I got back into the car he told me to look under the seat to get something and it was another card with a small box this time. I'm thinking that he was definitely going to propose but he didn't. It was another card stating how much he loved me with a diamond butterfly necklace in the small box.

I don't like surprises but he really did have me surprised. We were on our way to the second location and he would not tell me anything but to sit back and chill because the ride was going to be long. I guess that he didn't factor in that it was a Friday afternoon and traffic was thick. Our two-hour ride turned into 3½ hours and he was getting mad because it put us getting to Chateau Elan Winery & Resort pretty late and it was after dark, therefore we couldn't see the beautiful scenery when we pulled up.

I was definitely amazed at how huge the place was. It was like a castle on a lot of land. We got our things out and headed inside to check in. By this time, I had forgotten all about getting a ring because this place was so beautiful. When we walked into the room it was all white and elegant with rose petals on the bed in the shape of the heart with a bottle of champagne sitting next to the bed.

All of the sudden Damon gets down on one knee and say "I can't hold it in any longer. Shaletha Lynn, will you marry me?" Of course, I can't be normal, so I write "Yes" on a piece of paper. We hugged and kissed and went to our reserved dinner on site. Since it was late, we didn't have time to change clothes or freshen up because it was really close to our reservation time.

The next day we woke up and had breakfast before we got started with our day. Once again Damon had this day planned out as well. I was to go to the spa on the property while he goes to play golf. The set up was really nice. I was to get changed and go to the sauna first and relax, then go in another room for a luxurious mani and pedi. I felt weird not being with him when we just got engaged, but I tried to make the best of it alone. The nail area was amazing; it was definitely not anything I was used to. They gave me champagne with chocolate covered caviar. I was a little reluctant in eating it but my nail tech informed me that it was good. To my surprise, it was really good; didn't taste like what I heard about it.

This was such an awesome experience because I've never had anyone do anything like this for me before. I still had two hours left in the spa so I went and got a head and neck massage with a facial. I learned a lot about my face and what type of products I should use. I picked out some products for me to start using because I wasn't taking care of my face like I needed to since I was working outside every day.

Our time at Chateau Elan had come to an end and it was nothing but wonderful. I felt like a whole new person. I now know what being on cloud nine feels like. The last thing we did was wine tasting. It was an amazing and friendly atmosphere. That was my first-time wine tasting and trying new cheese. I really did enjoy the different tastes in my mouth. I was a little nervous because I don't like trying new things. Before we left, we walked around the huge beautiful property and took a lot of pictures.

The Marriage

As a child, I really didn't get to see love in a two-parent house. I wasn't taught the meaning of love. We didn't say I love you in our household, so therefore I didn't know how to apply love towards other people. With my family, we just knew that we loved each other. We took care of each other. We did everything together as a family and we were all very close, so there was no longing for love or the feeling to be loved.

I was taught to be loyal and take care of the ones you love. I was that ride or die chick. I would have your back no matter what. I was taught how to be independent and grind hard to get things for myself.

When Damon proposed to me I was like okay cool, this guy must really love me. I had my own house, my own car and I had more than enough money saved in my bank account with a 401K. And with me being almost thirty with no kids, I figured that this was the only thing missing in my life, so why not.

We set our wedding date for April 14, 2011, almost six months after he proposed to me. I didn't feel the need to have a long engagement because we were already living together. Those months went by super-fast; it was like I couldn't catch up. I was planning the wedding, looking for a venue and decorations all while working. Once we chose the colors, it was pretty simple. But Damon didn't like how busy I was running around so he suggested that we hire a wedding planner. At first I didn't agree to it because I had already done a lot but I understood. It does take a lot out of you.

I started looking for planners who would fit into our budget. We agreed that our honeymoon was more important than spending a lot of money on the wedding. We ended up going with this one lady who would do everything we wanted within our budget. She had a lot of decorations already so I was able to save on that and it allowed for us to get other things like the cake and bartender.

One month before the wedding I was diagnosed with type II diabetes at thirty years old. I was devastated because I loved to eat any and everything and watching what I ate was going to be so challenging for me. I really didn't know anything about it except that my grandmother had it. I had to study on it, take classes on it, see a diabetic doctor, and see a nutritionist. My life had literally changed overnight and I was due to go on an all-inclusive cruise the following month. How was I supposed to watch what I ate?

Two days before the wedding Damon's parents arrived and it was my first time meeting them in person. We had only talked on the phone since they lived in New York. Everything went great and we all got along good. It was very different for me having a house full of people because it had been just me for a long time. I got a room block close to where the wedding ceremony would be so that is where most of my family were staying for that weekend so I didn't see most of them until the wedding day.

Our Wedding Day

"For this reason a man will leave his father and mother and be united to his wife, and the two will become one flesh."
Ephesians 5:31 - NIV

I woke up not knowing what to expect. I am a nonchalant person so I was happy but not jumping out of my skin happy. I just wanted to make sure that I had everything, which I didn't. My friend and I stayed at the hotel the night before since they say you are not supposed to see the other person before the wedding. I had the whole day planned out with things to do. Our ceremony was not due to start until 4pm.

I got up, had breakfast and went to Salon B to get my hair done by my best friend who was my beautician at that time. My hair was down to my shoulders so it really didn't take long to do because the way she did it only gave it length, which was so pretty when she finished it. After the salon, I went to get my nails and toes done which took another couple of hours. Once I was done with that, I went to the mall to get my makeup done. That's where everyone told me to go and the person who was working the Mac counter told me that they don't do free makeup service, but she could do it for $50.

I left and went to the beauty supply store and got some lashes and makeup. Since I had even more time, I went to get Sexy Red washed (which was my Lexus). It was supposed to be a beautiful weekend. After that I checked all my items so that I could head to the venue and get ready which was in Newnan, Ga. Then I noticed that I didn't have my dress. OMG! I am way across town from where I lived and I needed my dress. I headed home pushing it. When I arrived there, the wedding party was getting ready to leave and was confused as to what I was doing there. Since I wasn't staying in my room, I totally forgot where I had put the dress and didn't grab it when I packed my bag for the hotel.

It was a Friday afternoon and traffic was getting bad on 285S going towards Newnan. I was pressed for time because I still needed to do my makeup. I arrived to the venue 1½ hour later and rushed in to find out that everything wasn't done yet. Damon's mom kept me away and told me to just worry about getting ready and they would take care of everything else. That was a hard task, but I did need to get ready.

What went wrong next, went wrong. I couldn't do my makeup right and I didn't know how to put the eyelashes on so I called one of my friends who were already there and asked her to help me and she stated that she didn't know how to do makeup and went and got our other friend to come and help. She was able to clean up what didn't look right and put my eyelashes on. I wasn't a pro like I am now or else it would have been all good.

Finally, I was ready to be escorted out. By this time everyone was waiting on me because I was 40 minutes behind schedule from having to get ready. My uncle met me at the front where I was to come in at and I got nervous and started to cry. What was happening to me? Was all I could think. He told me that it was normal for this to happen and I would be okay.

"But you must remain faithful to the things you have been taught. You know they are true, for you know you can trust those who taught you. You have been taught the Holy Scriptures from childhood, and they have given you the wisdom to receive the salvation that comes by trusting in Christ Jesus."
2 Timothy 3:14-15 -NLT

This was a very special moment for me because all of my family and friends were there and most importantly my grandmother officiated the wedding ceremony. I was in such a zone that I didn't realize the planner didn't have everything that we were supposed to have and we didn't have a wedding cake because she dropped it coming into the building. But the show must go on and our parents wouldn't allow me to address anything because it was our special day.

Damon and I were about to leave for the night and noticed that the wedding planner took the building key home with her. We called her to bring the key back and while we were waiting, the bartender came out to inform us that the planner didn't pay her. I told the planner that per our contract, she was supposed to pay the bartender and I was to take care of the photographer and the DJ and that's all I had money for.

Since we were waiting on her to come back, the bartender stayed so that she could get her money. Once the planner showed up, the bartender immediately started in on her about leaving and not paying her for her services. And then out of nowhere, the planner walked up to me and started in on me and pushing me. Who has a fight on their wedding day?! The men that were there grabbed her. She was like 300 pounds and plus, why are you fighting the bride?

The bartender called the police on her so that they could handle the situation. I ended up getting a ticket for fighting which was not my fault. Damon was so mad at me and didn't understand what happened because he was inside the building. I was trying to explain to him but he didn't want to hear it. He didn't say anything to me for the rest of the night or have sex with me. I thought that was strange because it was our wedding night and we hadn't had sex in a couple of weeks because that was a part of our marriage counseling.

Our first night as husband and wife was a complete failure and I didn't know what to think. I thought no matter what, he would have my back just like I would have his, but that wasn't the case.

Moving on With Our Lives

It had been a couple of months now since we've been married and things were going well. We were in the process of finding another home for us and making my house a rental home. Since Damon had two kids and both of our families were huge, he wanted to find a bigger house so that it would be enough room for everyone.

We found the perfect house for us and the perfect tenant for my home all within weeks of each other. I was like wow; God is really working everything out for us. Maybe I spoke too soon.

Three months later I was let go from my 6½ year job. I didn't know what to do because that job was my everything. I have learned so many things from working with that company. I had made so much money with that company that I was able to buy a house and car while working there. It was a battle but I was able to collect unemployment because the person that got me fired lied on me and they couldn't provide any proof against me. Most importantly, I had God on my side.

I didn't realize then but I had been praying for God to make a way for me to finish school because I really did want to become a medical biller and insurance coder. But with my work schedule I was not able to attend on-site classes, just do some of the school work online. I immediately enrolled in school for the fall season and just focused on that. I was able to transfer a lot of credits since I had attended college before. This course was only going to take me 9 months to finish.

I had money saved in the bank and I was getting unemployment so I wasn't too worried about finding a job. At that time Damon was okay with me not working and just focusing on school. He wanted me to be able to say that I didn't have to work; my husband takes care of everything. Well that lasted for so long. Something happened at his job and he was let go. To this day I still don't know what happened because it seemed like everything was going so good for him and he was the assistant manager over a store.

We found out that I was pregnant after being married only for five months. I was scared and didn't know what to do. I didn't want to have any kids because I didn't think that I would be a good mother. And I wasn't working so how would I provide for this child?

We were in complete shock because it seemed as if I couldn't get pregnant because we never used protection. After finding out, it seemed like Damon was just lost, like he just couldn't find his way. He started becoming distant and very short with me. The fighting and arguments started just because I would ask him questions. One night things got so bad between us that I had to hit him in the head with a glass to get him off of me.

He was holding me hostage in my own house and wouldn't let me go; hitting me for no reason. The next day when he left, I packed a bag and went to a hotel for the rest of the week because he took my keys the night before so that I couldn't go anywhere. I didn't know what to do or who to talk to so I left to be by myself.

Six months into my pregnancy, we went to visit my family in Texas. I think just to get a break from everyday life in Ga. Everything looked so different to me. It was like a whole new city. We were able to do some sightseeing and spend time with all of my family. It was a really good trip for us. Damon liked it so much that when we got back home he started applying for jobs in Texas just in case nothing worked out for him in Ga.

The craziest thing is that he was getting a lot of call backs from jobs in Texas than he was here in Atlanta. Once they found out that he didn't live there, a lot of them passed on him. Which had to be God because I ended up having my baby four weeks early at 4 pounds and 5 ounces. I was a little nervous because the month before the doctor told me that the baby had a hole in her heart. After that appointment I went home and started praying over my belly and baby declaring that we were God's children and He blessed me to get pregnant and nothing was going to happen to my baby.

When I went in for a doctor's appointment a month later on a Thursday and found out that my blood pressure was high and needed to go to the hospital for observation, I knew something wasn't right. I was swollen and come to find out that I had gained twenty pounds in one week. I went home and told Damon what was said at my appointment and packed a small bag and ate some food because I didn't know if I was going to be able to eat once I got to the hospital.

After all of the tests were ran, I ended up being diagnosed with preeclampsia which was causing my weight gain and high blood pressure. I am so thankful because I had my baby shower on the 12th and God allowed me to finish my internship the week before and I was due to graduate from college on May 22, 2012.

There were so many things going on and mixed emotions. Everything was happening so fast that I barely had time to take it all in. Once I told Damon what was going on he rushed up there to be with me. The doctor was able to get my blood pressure under control by inducing my labor. Since this was happening, Damon and I thought that it would be best if we told the family what was going on. It was a good thing that we did because baby Zina came two days later. They couldn't hear her heartbeat anymore and thought it was best to do an emergency C-section to make sure that she was okay.

My baby was perfect. I couldn't believe that I had just had a little baby girl. For years I didn't want any kids but once I felt her move in my stomach I fell in love with the idea even though I was scared because Damon was changing.

I was still a little out of it when they brought Zina to see me and all I could do was look her over to make sure that she had 10 fingers and 10 toes and asked about her heart and they said that it was whole and healthy as well as her lungs because she came out 4 weeks early at 4.5 pounds.

I broke down crying thanking the Lord for keeping my baby safe and helping her little body grow. The hospital had prepared us for the NICU and the worst but I knew better. I knew that God didn't bring me all this way to leave me. I was so overjoyed with happiness that they had to take her away.

Texas, Here We Come

One week after I had the baby Damon got a call from a company in Texas that was willing to offer him a job if he moved there. We talked about it and weighed his options and decided that was going to be the best move for our family. We called my grandmother and talked with her and asked if he could stay with her until he gets on his feet. Of course, she said yes.

We started letting everyone know that he was moving and then I was like, I want to move too. I wasn't working and I had just had a baby so therefore I wasn't going to be doing anything in Ga. We called my grandmother back and asked would it be okay if the three of us moved in with her for a little while and she was super excited for us to come.

My mom was a great help for us. She went to the house and washed up all of Zina's clothes before we were released from the hospital. I was truly blessed because the nurses gave me clothes, milk and diapers for the baby. I was so grateful because everything that we had received from the baby shower was too big for her since she was only four pounds.

My mom stayed with us for two weeks cooking and cleaning and watching Zina so that I could get some rest. The medication that I was on kept me sleepy, so I wouldn't have been much help to Zina anyway. Our friends and family took turns coming over to help out with the baby and to help us pack up the house we were living in even though they were sad that we were moving away with the baby. We still had everyone's support. Since I had a C-section, I wasn't much help so I just slept and watched Zina. I couldn't stop looking at her. I couldn't stop thanking God for her and asking Him to let me be a good mother because I had no clue on what to do.

Six years later I still sit back and watch her thanking God for blessing me with my precious daughter. Now I realize and understand what true love feels like. Besides loving God, I had never experienced that before.

Two days before our move we were in a good place and Damon was handling everything like moving our things into storage, selling items that we weren't going to use anymore and loading up our two cars for the 12-hour drive to Texas. Out of nowhere my mom had an issue with us moving but didn't say anything to us about it. She kept it in and started spreading rumors about us to my other family members. She even loaned Damon some money for our rent and I was the only one left in the dark.

I didn't know that he needed money because he was going to work every day and coming home like everything was okay. I was so hurt because I couldn't believe that they kept a secret from me and I didn't understand why he had to go outside of our home to ask someone else for money when I had the money. His excuse was that he didn't want to worry me while I was pregnant, I really didn't know how to respond to that because I thought that we were one, a team and was supposed to talk to each other about everything.

Clearly that wasn't the case. He wanted to keep everything separate and made me feel like I wasn't supposed to ask any questions or know anything that was going on with him. Since moving in with my grandma and grandpa, things stayed good for a while. We were doing everything together as a family. He spent all of his off days with us and we just spent that time getting to know Dallas.

We were in a really good place except money wise. Since he was new to the company he wasn't making a lot of money yet and I wasn't working yet because my sweet baby girl was only one month old. I did things around the house to help my grandmother out and I was always available to help with my grandfather. I am so thankful that Zina was able to get to know them in their last years.

Going Back to Work

Two and a half months of being in Texas just living in the house with a newborn, wasn't working for me. I decided that maybe it was time for me to go back to work after not working for a year. I started going on interviews and nothing was working out and plus I didn't know what I was going to do with baby Zina. Out of nowhere I got a call from a Chiropractor's office and set up an interview and got a call back the next day. I was excited that I was able to land a job and that my aunt said that she will keep Zina for a couple of months while I work and get myself together. I was so grateful for that because she even kept her for free and picked her up every morning from Damon.

I felt like life was finally looking out for me not knowing what lied ahead. A week later I started working and leaving my baby behind. It was such a different feeling for me. I never knew that I wouldn't want to go back to work because I loved to work, I had been working since I was 14 years old and needed that feeling of working and making my own money.

God had really been good to me so I was able to get an interview with one of the largest hospitals here in Dallas and the interviewer was impressed by me and sent my resume to two managers within a week. I actually got a call back from one of the managers and had an interview lined up with her and I was super nervous because the devil was getting in my head about my past. I discounted myself and the plan God had for me before I even went on the interview.

Work was going good; Zina and Damon were doing good and the interview went well so of course the devil had to try another route and this time it was with my mom. I wasn't sure what was going on or what the issue was but she stated that I was using her credit card and not paying down the balance. A couple of years back she added me onto one of her cards to help boost my credit because I didn't believe in using those. My motto was "if you couldn't pay cash for it, then you don't need it".

To make a long story short, I was paying off what I was using and it was like $40 left to pay so I paid it and cancelled the card. I wanted to make sure that I didn't have that problem again. She had an issue with me cancelling the card which I thought would be okay so that she didn't have to worry about it anymore. I guess that she wasn't satisfied with that solution and tried something else. A month later she came to Texas to visit and stayed with my aunt.

Since she didn't charge me to keep Zina, I would buy my Aunt groceries and drop them off when I picked up my daughter from her house. One particular day I went over there to get Zina and I walked in the house spoke and preceded to gather up Zina's things. Five minutes later the atmosphere changed and my mom just flipped out. Yelling and cursing at me and picked up a knife and tried to fight me.

I was so confused; we were all confused as to what was happening. I was really hurt by the situation because who wants to have a fight with their parents. She begins throwing my baby stuff outside on the street and telling me to get out of the house and that made me so mad because I was thinking how rude and what if my daughter was in her car seat?

Everything was happening so fast that I threw something at her to try and stop her from coming at me and my aunt told me to just go outside that she would bring my baby out to the car. I gathered all of Zina's thing off the ground and got in the car. I think this was my first time ever experiencing an anxiety attack. I didn't know what was going on or what had just happened so I called my husband frantic telling him what just happened and to come home now.

"Father in heaven, thank you for loving me and telling me that you are enough. Thank you for breaking down the lies that the enemy has told.

Thank you for your perfect love that drives out fear that the devil has planted. In Jesus name, Amen!"

God's Doing A New Thing

We tried to move on with our lives like it was before, but a couple of days later after that incident, my aunt called me to say that she wasn't going to keep Zina for me anymore and that I needed to figure it out.

I couldn't believe what I was hearing because we never had an issue with one another and she was the one that offered to keep Zina so that I could work. But me being me I didn't ask any questions and just said "okay".

I went to work the next morning a zombie because I didn't know what to do and I didn't want to sit at home and not work. Eventually we were planning on moving out from my grandmother's house.

As the months went on, Damon and I stayed to ourselves. We didn't know who to trust anymore. It felt like it was us against the world. We began going to my grandmother's church and I started back praying to God for guidance.

I had been on interviews but no one was calling me back. And I started to get discouraged and wondered if it was because of my background. God began to speak to me about him changing my name and providing a different life for me. At that time, I didn't really understand what that meant.

Then boom! God showed up like He always does to take care of His child. I got a call from one of the largest hospitals here in Dallas for a job offer. I was so excited that I didn't get any information from the hiring manager. I didn't know where I was working, I didn't know how much I was getting paid and I didn't know what my work hours was going to be.

The church that we were going to had an on-site daycare and God showed up again. It was last minute but He allowed them to accept Zina and at an affordable rate. I was so grateful since I didn't have anyone to keep her anymore.

Finally, I was working after being off for a year and a couple of months I was about to go crazy because I had never been off work for this long. I had been working since I was fourteen years old. Since I was still getting unemployment from my previous job, I was able to buy me some work clothes and shoes for the week. I had been doing valet parking for six years and all that I had were uniforms and tennis shoes.

Man, waking up in the morning for work is totally different from waking up when I wanted to or when the baby was crying. It took me about three weeks to get used to waking up at 6am to get ready and drive to work. There was no more sitting alone in the back office until I woke up. There was no more talking to people after 10am because once the clinic opened at 8 o'clock, the patients' area was full.

I still couldn't believe that I got a job working with the state. I was so grateful to God for giving me this opportunity that I wanted to make sure that He knew. I went in everyday and did my best at that job. I went above and beyond to learn everything that I could work in that clinic and once my benefits kicked in I went to every doctor that I could to get checked out.

Since I worked in the OB/GYN department it was easy for me to start there. I went for all of my female needs because I hadn't been checked out since I had the baby. And then I was able to get referrals for the other doctors that I needed to see like an orthopedic doctor.

Two years before I had the baby, I started to have lower back and leg pain. I thought that since I was in a car accident that was the root cause of it. I began to go to the chiropractor to get adjustments and it helped relieve some pain so therefore I was able to keep functioning.

I will never forget in January 2013, I saw the orthopedic doctor and he looked at my x-rays. He was like "ok Mrs. Marshall, you have Osteonecrosis of the hip and you're at stage 4 so therefore we need to go ahead and do a total left hip replacement." I was in complete shock because I was not expecting to hear what came out of his mouth. I had so many questions, I actually thought that he was joking and laughed at him. Me, have a bone disease? How is this possible? I'm only 32 and I've never heard of this before and no one in my family has this.

The doctor continued going over everything with me and stated that it's okay, this type of disease happens to people in their 30's. But that didn't help ease my concern. I told him that I had just started working there and that I was not going to be able to take off work just yet.

I went home and talked it over with my family because I was still confused and had questions as to why was I having this pain and no one else? After taking everything in and thinking how I wouldn't be in pain anymore and how I would be able to play with my baby once she started crawling and no more walking with a limp at age 32.

I was praying to God that I needed to hear a word from Him. I was so confused because two years ago I was diagnosed with type-two diabetes and married one month later. I could not figure out what did I do wrong to deserve all that I was going through. The Lord said to me that He blessed me with that job and gave me a new name, a new identity so that I could get the help that I needed and not to worry about anything.

Besides having Zina, I had never been in the hospital before and was super nervous, because I had heard that once you get cut open, different things could happen to your body.

> ***"Behold, the former things have come to pass, Now I declare new things; Before they spring forth I proclaim them to you."***
> ***Isaiah 42:9 –NASB***

About a month later, the clinic called me to tell me that everything was approved and when would I like to schedule the surgery. I was like wait, what, approved? What about my job, how much does this cost? The nurse told me to calm down because they handled everything and would let my job know that I would need to be off.

Jezebel Spirit

Jennifer LeClaire talks about the 7 Indicators of a Jezebel Spirit in her book.

- People influenced by a spirit of Jezebel have fear issues of rejection. They control others so that they will not be hurt.

- They target the headship. They offer free help to be their top assistant because they want their protection. It hides from the leader's view but manifests in front of others.

- They make commitments and promises quickly and use recommendations from others to impress others.

- They seem super-spiritual in an exaggerated way to gain acceptance and attention. They have their own agenda. They are looking for disciples of their own.

- They isolate and pit people against each other privately and individually behind closed doors.

- They play the victim. They are never wrong. They blame everyone else. They play on compassion to block discernment.

- They use false humility and feel entitled or owed something.

Things have definitely changed within our household. I could not figure out what was going on, but I knew that something was off. One night in

2014, I was sleeping and all of a sudden, I was waking up to people talking or so I thought. The craziest thing is that I couldn't move or talk but my eyes were open. And then I began to hear someone walking towards me and I tried to yell out to my husband but no words came out. This was the first time in my life that I was really scared of something. I closed my eyes because I did not want to see what was coming. The closer the presence came towards me, the closer I could hear the whispers. I tried my best to get up so that I could turn the light on to see who or what was in my room but I was completely paralyzed.

I kept my eyes closed and I began to pray and repent for all my sins and ask God to help me through whatever it was that I was experiencing and to keep me safe because I did not know or understand what was going on. This encounter felt like it lasted for about 20 minutes. I could feel tears rolling down my face and then I just felt this sense of relief. There were no more whispering, everyone was gone and I was able to move again.

The next morning, I woke up with my body feeling tight like I was in a fight. Wondering why I was feeling that way and then I remembered what happened in my sleep. I went online and typed in what I remembered. That's when I read about sleep paralysis, which is the feeling of being conscious but unable to move. I also read that sometimes there is an "evil" presence that will come or "night demons" from fear that will try to terrorize you. I immediately put my phone down and went and got my bless oil and began to pray over my house. Touching all the windows, doors and door knobs. Casting out all types of demons that may have been there. That situation has never happened again.

"Many will say to me on that day, 'Lord, Lord, did we not prophesy in your name and in your name drive out demons and in your name perform many miracles?"
Matthew 7:22 -NIV

Damon was dishonest about finances and where a portion of his money was going. He wanted to keep his finances separate from mine so he had his own bank account. When we first got married we opened up a joint account to put money in for monthly bills and savings. Well, let's just say that didn't work. He was using all the money for little items and stupid things so I stopped putting my money into that account. Within three months he had negative charges of $300. After that I was like okay this is definitely not the route for us. We agreed that he would just give me money monthly for bills.

In 2015, we started our own credit repair business and things were going good but I just couldn't figure out how was it that we were bringing in almost $10k a month between the both of us and had nothing to show for it? I was handling the clients' paperwork on a daily basis and making sure that payments were coming in monthly so I knew how much the business was making. This particular time I asked him about the money, he instantly got angry at me and stated that "this is my business and my money so therefore it has nothing to do with you so don't ask me about my money."

I said you're right this is your business and I won't do anything else with it. I was busting my butt trying to make sure that we had a household with five streams of income coming in so that we wouldn't have to work for anyone else and he wanted to be selfish. I was working my full-time job and would come home to work our other businesses. And I had to give that over to God because I wasn't going to argue, fuss and fight with him.

Then God began to show me things about us or shall I say about him and I would be like Damon, God said this, God said that. Damon God is waiting on you to do something before He releases everything that He has in store for us. But he never took heed to my warnings. He made me feel like I wasn't doing things right. The devil began to plant lies in my head and I began to feel insecure about myself. I begin to question myself because he told me that I had issues and this or that was wrong with me. He made me feel like everything I said or did was wrong. I didn't know who I was anymore because I was so consumed with trying to figure out what was happening right before my eyes.

I began to lose interest in my marriage. I just didn't like my husband anymore and I didn't like having sex with him anymore. He began to what felt like rape me. He knew how I felt about having sex against my well because I was raped in high school by two boys that I did not know.

He knew how I felt when pinned down, penetrating me while I was crying telling him to stop and he never would until he was finished. He knew how I felt to have him jabbing me knowing that my vagina was not producing any moisture and it would always feel like this burning, tearing of my vagina and sometimes bleeding during and after sex.

He told me that there was something wrong with me. I ended up going to three different doctors trying to figure out why I didn't like having sex anymore, not knowing that it was all stemming from within my home. I was 33 years old and wanted to know why did sex hurt and was very uncomfortable when I knew deep down that I loved to have sex. My doctor started testing me for early stages of menopausal. For two months straight I was having all types of tests done and everything came back negative.

Every time we were intimate I would get sick. I thought that to be strange, but hey I didn't know any different. And for the life of me I could not figure out what was wrong. It seemed like the more I tried to talk to him the more he became angry and evil looking towards me. Damon had definitely taken his mask off. I continued to be nice and loving but I was just not happy, my soul was not happy. How can you be married and still feel single? How can you be married and feel alone at the same time?

> **"If anyone thinks himself to be religious, and yet does not bridle his tongue but deceives his own heart, this man's religion is worthless. Pure and undefiled religion in the sight of our God and Father is this: to visit orphans and widows in their distress, and to keep oneself unstained by the world."**
> **James 1:26-27 -NASB**

At this point I began to seek out God because I knew that He was the only one that could help me. One of my friends suggested that I read the book "The Power of a Praying Wife" by Stormie Omartian. Once I started to read it, I couldn't stop. I began to apply those things she mentioned in her book to my life. I realized that I was going about things all wrong, but I didn't have anyone to give me sound advice.

My church didn't seem like they cared about family personal lives as long as they were still coming and serving in the church. After three months of reading, fasting and praying, my mind and thought process began to change and I no longer gave negative energy to the marriage. I was seeking the Lord to change me and renew my mind.

> *"I know your works, love, service, faith, and your patience; and as for your works, the last are more than the first. Nevertheless, I have a few things against you, because you allow that woman Jezebel, who calls herself a prophetess, to teach and seduce My servants to commit sexual immorality and eat things sacrificed to idols."*
> **Revelation 2:19-20 -NKJV**

God began to speak to me and reveal dreams to me, but I didn't quite fully understand what they meant. I stayed active in church and serving God like nothing was happening in my home. It seemed like the more I prayed and got into the word, the more Damon became angry spirited. His whole demeanor was changing and I didn't like being around him anymore. I tried to stay away from him as much as I could.

I would pick my daughter up from school and we would hang out, go out or if he picked her up from school I would go sit at the park and read. Sometimes I would go to the movies by myself just so that I could have some peace. Because all he wanted to do was argue and I was constantly telling him to stop yelling at me for every little thing. It seemed like every Sunday he would pick a fight with me. We even started taking separate cars to church. I couldn't ride with him anymore because the yelling and cursing me out would alter my mood for church. I couldn't wrap my head around how this minister was treating his own wife. I knew that it wasn't right but I had no one I could talk to and figured that if I kept going to church that things would get better.

Then the pushing began and he began to do it in front of my daughter. One time we were in our bedroom talking about something stupid like always and then out of nowhere Zina said "daddy stop yelling at my momma, let her go." I knew right then that our marriage was coming to an end. I didn't know how or what was going to happen but I knew being in that relationship was not healthy for me or my child.

The mental abuse and emotional abuse were starting to take a toll on me. I didn't like being in that situation and I definitely didn't want my daughter being exposed to that type of environment. That's when I cried out to the Lord to help me with this situation because at this point man couldn't do anything for me. This wasn't love, this wasn't Agape Love that my God promised me to have.

"Lord this is not what marriage is about. This is not how your word say marriage is supposed to look like. This is not how I wanted my marriage to be. I knew that I did this without you but God there has to be more to life than this. Lord I'm so tired of always feeling like I'm not good enough. Lord I'm tired of feeling like I don't belong here in my own house. Lord I'm tired of feeling like I'm not doing enough or anything right.' And who knew what would happen a couple of months later. "

Who's Baby

Two days before Mother's Day 2016, I received a call on my work phone from this girl telling me information about my husband Damon. I wasn't quite sure on what she was telling me so I told her to hold while I get some paper and a pen because I had just got back to my desk from lunch when the phone rang.

I asked her what the call was about again and she stated, "She was calling me to let me know that Damon was not paying her child support" and I asked what was the support for and she said, "For his son." I said "okay thank you. I will relay the message to him." Before we got off the phone she was like don't call him, call me back before you mention anything to him. After that everything was a blur.

Our marriage wasn't perfect, but it wasn't that bad. Never in a million years would I have thought that Damon was cheating on our family and had another family on the side. I didn't understand how this happened because he was home every day sometimes doing the cooking and cleaning. I couldn't believe that a man of God would do something like this. He was a minister; we were active in church and going to church every time the doors were open.

When I called Damon to tell him what happened, he acted as if he was shocked, but lied to me at the same time. He stated that was a bogus call and why would someone call me at work to tell me those things. You know how they say you reap what you sow. I figured all those years of using men for money and talking to married men was coming back to bite me. But what I couldn't get over was him having a 6-month-old baby, being on child support and never saying anything to me because we were trying to have another baby at that time.

> ***"God is not holding you hostage for what you did in your past."***
> **–Pastor Todd**

I really couldn't wrap my head around the situation and why God allowed this to happen to me. I couldn't sleep, I couldn't eat and I could barely take care of my child. This was the first time in my life that I fell into a depression and wanted to kill myself. I had a reduced appetite and weight loss. I couldn't concentrate or remember things. I felt like a walking zombie. I didn't know if I was coming or going.

The headaches wouldn't go away, my mind wouldn't stop racing and I didn't want to be married anymore. I had no more joy. My home was not peaceful anymore because all I wanted to do was hurt something.

One day when I was coming home from work, I pulled into the garage like normal and cracked my windows just thinking that if I could just go to sleep everything would be better; I would feel better about life. But that didn't happen. That day God allowed Damon to be home and he came into the garage and took the keys out of the ignition. After that he was like we need to go to counseling to get our marriage back on track. I agreed.

This Feels Like Death

Death means the action or fact of dying or being killed; the end of the life of a person or organism. That's exactly what it felt like when Damon packed up his stuff and left. I didn't know how to feel or understand what was going on because we had no discussion about our marriage being over or him moving out.

He left 3 days before our home was scheduled for foreclosure in December 2016. I had so many questions. Lord why me? Lord what did I do wrong? Lord what was I supposed to do? I felt so lost and confused because I couldn't believe that this happened to me and I had this little girl looking up at me telling me that it's okay. Everything will be fine.

One day my aunt reminded me of Job in the bible and how he went through a lot of things in life and how he was abundantly wealthy and God took it all away from him. Once Job realized that all he needed to do was repent for his sins and submit himself unto the Lord and stop fighting God about the problems he was facing and accept them as is, the Lord restored him with even more then he could ever imagine.

> *"But he said to her, "You speak as one of the foolish women speaks. Shall we indeed accept good from God, and shall we not accept adversity?" In all this Job did not sin with his lips."*
> **Job 2:10 -NKJV**

The bible states that God showed Job favor and at the end God blessed him with even more than he ever had before; that gave me hope. I needed to be like Job and remember that "the Lord gives and the Lord takes away." After I got over the initial shock, I cried out to God for about three hours and asked him to help me get over this situation and to help me take care of my daughter.

"And the Lord restored Job's losses when he prayed for his friends. Indeed, the Lord gave Job twice as much as he had before. Then all his brothers, all his sisters, and all those who had been his acquaintances before, came to him and ate food with him in his house; and they consoled him and comforted him for all the adversity that the Lord had brought upon him. Each one gave him a piece of silver and each a ring of gold. Now the Lord blessed the latter days of Job more than his beginning; for he had fourteen thousand sheep, six thousand camels, one thousand yoke of oxen, and one thousand female donkeys. He also had seven sons and three daughters. And he called the name of the first Jemimah, the name of the second Keziah, and the name of the third Keren-Happuch. In all the land were found no women so beautiful as the daughters of Job; and their father gave them an inheritance among their brothers."
Job 42:10-15 -NKJV

"Father God, I come to you today asking for forgiveness for my questioning you about my life's circumstances. I know that you have a plan for me and need me to get back on track. Help me to accept the situation for what it is with your loving grace. Right now, father I just ask you to bring peace over my life. Amen!"

Broken Promises

I believe that every couple has problems, but I do know that they can be fixed or worked through. And I know that God can restore a marriage if you put in the work and if it's God's will for that marriage. I remember Damon telling me after we got married that divorce was not an option this time around. Because this was his second marriage and he knew now what he wanted out of life and a family.

In my mind we had the perfect little family. Even though I didn't think about marriage or kids beforehand, the three of us were good together. I didn't grow up with my father so I didn't know what the father daughter bond looked like until I had my daughter. Once I was over the marriage, I did not want to take that away from her.

Damon never said that he was sorry or explained what happened to make him leave his family. But he did say that he would help me by continuing to take Zina to school so that I could keep going to work at my regular time.

I know that was nothing but God. Seeing that when he first left, he was not talking to me. He was mean and rude to me. Like I was the one that cheated on him and made him leave. That first week he was gone it was rough and I was trying to get my life together but the anxiety wouldn't stop and I went into a depression.

The negative thoughts wouldn't leave my head. There were feelings of worthlessness, being a failure and self-blame of what I could have done differently. I was feeling very sad, empty and hopeless. I could not stop crying, I wasn't eating, I had a loss of interest and just couldn't get out of bed. I ended up using some of my vacation time at work to sit at home to be by myself.

Two months later, Damon said that since he messed everything up that he was going to find a place for Zina and I. In the meantime, he would work on my credit since I put a lot of things in my name so that he could get the house in his name.

Which, that never happened. He also told me that he would provide me with money to help me move since I had the down payment loan in my name. He was all talk but no actions. He only cared about himself and what he was trying to do. And God told me to be still. But I'm like how God? And He kept on telling me to be still. Once I surrendered that situation over to God I didn't have any more worries or anxieties about where Zina and I were going to live or how I was going to pay rent.

God said that He would use my brokenness to get the glory. He had to change things up so that I wouldn't depend on man any longer. He assured me that He would fight my battles. He assured me that He would supply all of my needs.

"Be still, and know that I am God; I will be exalted among the nations, I will be exalted in the earth!"

Psalm 46:10 - NKJV

Getting My Life Together

I began going to counseling to help get an understanding of what my life has become. At this time, I really didn't have anyone to talk to and I really didn't know anyone who went through the things that I was going through. Since Dr. Matthew helped us when we were going through the situation with me finding out that he was cheating and had a baby, I figured that I would continue to go to him since he knew my history.

When I had my first single session, Dr. Matthew was in complete shock by the things that I was telling him. He couldn't believe that Damon had packed up his things and left us, because just last year he was in Dr. Matthew's office crying about what happened and thinking that I would leave him for lying and cheating.

I wanted to heal from this situation. I didn't want the bitterness and hatred for Damon to linger on any longer because this was not only hurtful, it was affecting my health as well. I started to believe the lies that the devil planted in my head that I would never love again. No one would ever love you. How are you going to find a good man with a child? I told myself that I would hate Damon forever because of what he put us through.

I didn't want to continue taking depression medication because I knew that God could heal you from anything. It is okay to seek out help because you can't do it alone. God allowed me to realize that forgiveness was the only way to be free. I began to lay hands on myself and speak life into my mind and body, "I will live and not die. I will be happy again. Lord I forgive him even though I don't know what happened. Father I forgive him even though I may not ever get an apology". Telling God all the promises He made to me. Asking God to take away the spirit of fear. Take away the spirit of depression. And most importantly, take away the bitterness I have in my heart for Damon. And day by day I was set free from all those things that were holding me and my spirit hostage. And you too can be set free if you just allow God to help you get your life in order.

"Get rid of all bitterness, rage and anger, brawling and slander, along with every form of malice. Be kind and compassionate to one another, forgiving each other, just as in Christ God forgave you."
Ephesians 4:31-32 -NIV

One day I was looking on Facebook for a group that could possibly help me with what I was going through and came across this group called "Married and Young." I wasn't active in the group because I was trying to figure out if I was still married or not. I had no answers and no guidance on what to do or how to handle this situation.

I thought that I was not fulfilling my purpose in life and all I kept wondering was what happened and why me? God began to reveal things to me that helped me see our marriage totally differently and how He has better plans for me and where He was trying to take me, Damon couldn't go. My father had to strip me of things that were not of Him. He had to break me in ways that I could be free from the sin I chose to be in. I stopped questioning Him about the marriage and asking why me when He clearly stated, "Why not you?"

After going through those courses and breaking the cycle challenge, I do not want to pass anything to my daughter if I can help it. I wanted to become healed and whole for my Father to use me in my new season. I had to break all soul ties in my life; Lord knows that it was a lot. I realized that I was not putting God first in my life. My family had become my life without me even realizing it. Now I have the knowledge and understanding of what a Godly relationship and marriage should look like.

Meeting My Ishmael

It had been 6 months since my husband left me and I was in a really good place. Not being around Damon was like a breath of fresh air. I have peace in my life like I've never had before. There was no more of him coming over whenever he felt like it. No more coming over looking in my fridge seeing what food I had. And there was no more of him trying to have sex with me. I felt so free and clean since I was not having sex with him anymore.

Since Zina was gone for the summer I changed the locks on the house so that I could feel more comfortable. I didn't like how he would come over and stay the night sometimes. Even though I forgave him with God and wasn't bitter anymore, I still thought that he was disgusting. How could you be married with a family and have sex with all these women and come home and still have sex with me? And to make matters worse, he didn't feel that he did anything wrong.

I had taken this time to focus on God and continually thank Him for keeping me safe from any diseases. Even though I did get sick a couple of times from being intimate with Damon, it's nothing compared to what I could have caught if I wasn't covered by the grace of God.

I changed the way I ate and began working out 5 - 6 times a week. I was loving the new me and who I was becoming. I could feel God changing me and renewing my mind. People would say "wow, you are doing good. If this were me, I would still be mad." People would ask me "how are you going through a divorce and looking beautiful?" I would tell them that it was by the grace of God by showing me that I am His daughter, that I am here for a reason and that I am fearfully and wonderfully made.

> *"I will praise You, for I am fearfully and wonderfully made; Marvelous are Your works, And that my soul knows very well."*
> **Psalm 139:14 -NKJV**

I began going out with my friends with all the free time that I had. I didn't have a care in the world and that's when I began to enjoy my life in true happiness. My home had become peaceful after Damon and all of his evil spirits left. Even my 4-year-old daughter at the time noticed a difference in our home.

I was trying to rediscover myself and my purpose in life. After a couple of months hanging out, it just wasn't fun for me anymore. Not one guy tried to talk to me. I didn't get asked out on dates. No one asked to pump my gas. No one asked to buy my groceries. And guys weren't knocking down my door to get to me. I began to question myself because I knew that I was looking cute and kept myself up.

That's when I started learning that God will keep His chosen children hidden. Hidden means to keep out of sight; conceal from the view or notice of others. And that's what was happening to me. I had to accept the season that God had me in. God made me invisible to men. And shortly after, I had no desire to go anywhere that wasn't related to God and learning his word.

> *"And I will give thee the treasures of darkness and hidden riches of secret places, that thou mayest know that I, the Lord, which call thee by thy name, am the God of Israel."*
> **Isaiah 45:3 - KJV**

But God had other plans or shall I say the devil. I began to look into options of purchasing a home for myself and Zina and I just needed a couple of things removed from my credit since Damon never helped me. The loan officer I was working with referred my information to this credit repair company that he used. Weeks went by and I forgot all about it thinking that maybe it wasn't my time yet. One night out of nowhere this guy calls me.

Since I don't give my number out I didn't answer the phone when Bryan called. The second time he called he left a voicemail and I was able to call him back, and he explains why he was calling. We set up an appointment time for him to call me back and go over my credit repair options.

Two days went by and Bryan called me while I was at work and he began telling me about the program and what they can do for me. I explained to him my situation and how I ended up in this situation and what I was looking to gain from being in the program. I politely told Bryan that I didn't have the money at the time to start the program and he said that he would go ahead and get me set up and I could just pay him back when I could.

And that's when the conversation changed. I have talked to plenty of people in my life and this was the first time that someone who didn't know me or know how I looked asks if they could pray for me. I was caught completely off guard so I asked him what did he just say, and he said "I asked if I could pray for you?" Now that did something to me, those words touched my heart and mind in a way that I never felt before and I began to cry.

Who was this man? What did he want from me? Because throughout my years of dating, men always wanted something. And then those words escaped my mouth and it caught him off guard. He said "Mrs. Marshall I don't want anything from you, I don't even know you, but it is something about you makes me sad about how your situation is."

By this time, we had been on the phone for over four hours talking about any and everything. I told him that I really needed to go and get some work done. He then asked me if he could call me again because I sounded nice over the phone. I was a little skeptical at first because at this point I didn't trust anyone and I wasn't looking for anyone. Besides, I haven't conversed with the opposite sex in eight years.

We began talking over the phone and he was saying all the right things. I began to question God because it was like he was speaking to my heart with conversation. One afternoon he asked if he could see me and that's when anxiety kicked in. I was super nervous and told him no, I was not looking for anyone. I was in a really good place and had my own routine going. I didn't want anything to change in my life at that moment. But Bryan was so persistent. He even told me that if I was uncomfortable, I could just leave.

Since it was going to be a networking event with other people around I figured that nothing bad could happen and I would be in my own car so therefore I could leave whenever I wanted to. Luckily I had just done my hair the week before. All I had to do was figure out what to wear. I finally agreed to meet him later that night.

I arrived at the building and then I realized that I didn't know who I was meeting and immediately called him to inform him that I was there. And he was like okay great, I'm outside so I can meet you at your car. He described to me what he had on and looked like. I was super nervous. I didn't tell him what type of car I was in so that I could see him first. And when I tell you Bryan looked like an angel sent from heaven. He was just stunning. Very well groomed and dressed.

Instantly I was like God is this a trick, you pranking me right? I know that this man doesn't look this good. He definitely didn't look like how he sounded over the phone. His physical appearance was everything that I liked. He was perfect in my eyes. Bryan was 6'1 tall, medium built, light skinned with hazel eyes and bald headed. Amazingly fine! I just knew that God was joking with me. My mind was going 50 miles a minute. How was this breathtaking man single with no kids? Is this really happening? Will I finally have the man of my dreams? Okay Shaletha, snap out of it, we are just meeting to say hi.

Bryan introduced himself and said "wow you are so beautiful." I started blushing and he said "that is funny, I've never seen a browned skinned person turn red before." He was very observant, he noticed everything about me. He told me how pretty my smile was and that I had beautiful teeth. He even complimented me on the shoes that I was wearing that night.

We began to walk around talking as he introduced me to people at the event. Everything just flowed like we had known each other for months. I didn't want to come off as clingy so I told him that I would walk around and pass out my business cards.

As the night was getting late, he walked me to my car and we hugged each other goodbye. He asked "are you sure that your husband left you? Because you are so pretty and I can't believe that," I laughed. I thought that he was joking and I said "of course I am sure, why would I lie about something like that?" He said that he wanted to make sure and asked if he could call me. I wanted to scream "Hell Yeah You Can!"

I drove home in disbelief that a man with this type of stature would be interested in me. Then the negative thoughts started flooding my mind, 'who are you, you have nothing, you have baggage, you have a child, you are broken and your credit is bad.' While believing those lies from the enemy, I said "God if this is not of you, he will not call me."

The next day Bryan sends me a good morning Queen text. I wasn't sure of what that meant so I called my friend to ask her. In my 36 years I had never heard anyone call me that. I had never heard my mom refer to herself as a Queen or use the term King. I immediately thought that he was trying to run game on me.

"Now Sarai, Abram's wife, had borne him no children. But she had an Egyptian slave named Hagar; so she said to Abram, "The Lord has kept me from having children. Go, sleep with my slave; perhaps I can build a family through her." Abram agreed to what Sarai said. So after Abram had been living in Canaan ten years, Sarai his wife took her Egyptian slave Hagar and gave her to her husband to be his wife." Genesis 16:1-3 -NIV

I must say, he did have a way with his words and that is how he won his way into my heart. Bryan knew all the right things to say. It was like he knew that I had never been talked to in this type of manner before and that's how the soul tie was created without my knowledge. We began talking every day. He made me feel like a woman again. He made me feel beautiful and sexy. Bryan always complimented me on everything. He was giving me life in a new way.

A week and a half went by since we last saw each other and he wanted to see me. Zina was at home so I couldn't leave the house and meet him, but I did tell him that he could come over. At first he was not feeling that because my husband still had access to the house, but I assured him that he didn't come over anymore and that Zina would stay in the room watching TV, while we would be up front visiting with each other.

Later that evening Bryan took an Uber over. He said that was just in case he needed to run out of the back door if my husband came over. Once again I assured him that Damon does not come over so he would be safe. We sat upfront talking about how our day went. I could not stop smiling. I couldn't believe that this attractive looking man was sitting with me in my home. Compared to Damon, it was like looking at Ugli fruit (which is known as a Jamaican tangelo having rough, wrinkled skin) and the Pitaya (which is known as the dragon fruit or pearl fruit.)

Come to find out we had a lot of things in common. We liked to do similar things and we liked a lot of the same foods. It helped that he was one year older than me so he knew what he wanted out of life. He knew how to communicate with a woman. He knew his purpose and where God was taking him. I was instantly drawn to this man. He made me feel so comfortable around him. He would always refer to me as his Queen. We talked every day on the phone no matter what time it was. If he went out of town to work he made sure that he would check in on me.

After six months of not having sex or being intimate with the opposite sex, my body began to wake up. Kissing me goodnight before he left my house left me feeling like I had butterflies in my stomach. That was the first time in my life that I felt like I was actually melting. My flesh wanted this man desperately but I had to keep myself under control. I didn't want him to think anything less of me. I figured that if we would let some time go by without us seeing each other, those feelings would go away, but they didn't.

The next time I saw him was at his place to watch the game and later that night we ended up having sexual immorality and I was a lost cause after that. My body began to crave him and want him in every way possible instantaneously. Another soul tie was formed because of this physical act. I was vulnerable around him in a way that I had never experienced before and I didn't like it. I didn't like the connection that we had or that I wasn't in control of my thoughts any longer. The discernment that I once had was shattered when I met Bryan or should I say Ishmael in person. I did not realize that the devil plotted his way into my life to distract me from staying on God's course. I thought that I had truly found my ordained husband.

The months that I spent with him were by far the best time that I had than in my entire marriage. He made me feel wanted. He made me feel loved. And he made me feel important. He made me feel smart, none of the things that I received from Damon. Here I was once again giving man all my time, attention and love while putting my Father on the back burner. And one day God began to download on me all the things about myself that I was doing wrong.

Daddy said to me, "Shaletha you are still married what do you think you are doing," of course I replied back. "Lord, Damon left me. Damon is the one that cheated and Damon is the one that had a baby and covered it up. So why can't I talk to someone?" I heard Abba's voice clear as day tell me that I was committing adultery and what makes my sin better than Damon's?

I fell to my face and began weeping, telling my Father who has been so good to me that I was sorry and please forgive me for my sins and what did I need to do to fix it and get back right with you?

That's when the Lord told me to leave Bryan alone because he was a counterfeit, he was not my husband. I asked the Lord was there another way because I didn't want to stop seeing Bryan, and He said NO! The more we talked the more God demanded from me. He also told me to start back wearing my wedding ring because no matter what the situation is at the moment, I was still married and needed to carry myself as a married woman.

Talk about a blow to the gut. That really did hurt my feelings but I knew that He was right and I valued my Father's opinion more than any man. Since I am not good with letting people go, I just stopped talking to Bryan with no warning. He would call and text me but I would give no response back.

After a month went by I felt really bad for doing Bryan like that because of everything that he did for me. I asked the Lord to let him know and to give him an understanding of what happened and why we are not talking anymore. Then two days later I received a text from Bryan stating that God has been talking to him and that he understands and will listen. When I tell you that God is so good, He is awesome in every way possible. Receiving that text was like a load lifted off of my shoulders. Even though I was doing what God wanted me to do however, I do care about people's feelings.

Despite the fact that things didn't work out between us, I was able to laugh again. I was able to love again and I was able to enjoy sex again knowing that it was nothing wrong with me all those years. Bryan showed me what a real man was like intellectually, emotionally and spiritually. There was no belittling me, manipulation and playing word games. He gave me hope in knowing that I deserve better, I am worth better, and that I can have better which is God's best.

Becoming abstinent from sex again was like a breath of fresh air. I couldn't believe that I gave into temptation like that after not having sex for almost a year. Being with someone was the furthest thing from my mind. Initially I didn't realize the pattern because everyone else was so different. But I could tell that I was falling back into the cycle of neglecting God and making man my idol.

> *"Do not turn to idols or make for yourselves molten gods; I am the Lord your God."*
> **Leviticus 19:4 -NASB**

What Kind of Man Are You?

By this time, it was close to a year that Damon left and I wasn't getting any support from him. One Tuesday afternoon when I picked Zina up from school we went to his job to see if he would give us a little money for food and gas until I got paid the following month. When he saw me walk through the door it was like he had seen a ghost.

I began explaining to him that I needed some help financially because paying for Zina's before and after school program was taking a lot of my money. He didn't seem to care. He didn't care that he left us in a bad situation. He didn't care that I had to pawn half of my things so that we could have money for food. He didn't care that I was selling some of Zina's things to have gas money. He didn't care that I helped take care of his other children for almost 8 years whenever they came and stayed with us. And he didn't care that I helped him pay his car note for two months after he left us.

He gave me $40 and basically told me bye and to never come to his job again. I wanted to get mad at him for the way he treated us. But I had this peace over me. It was like God was saying don't worry my child you have been a good steward and vengeance is mine. We left and got something to eat. Afterwards we went to the store to get some tissue because we had been out for a week and was using paper towels.

I guess Damon was feeling some type of way after seeing that Zina was so happy to see him since he hasn't seen her in a couple of months, he texted me to pick her up the following weekend. Of course, he could I am not going to stop him from spending time with her because I know that's all she wants anyway. It seemed as if he was in a good mood so I asked him could he help pay for her daycare. At first he said yes and asked me how much it was and could he pay over the phone? I told him to let me check and see because I pay monthly online. I called him back to tell him that you can only pay in person if you were not registered with their organization.

And that's when his attitude changed and he said that he wasn't going to give me any money and that I would never get money from him. Which was weird to me because he wasn't giving me money and hasn't given my anything since he left in 2016. Then he proceeds to tell me that he was keeping Zina until she was 18 years old since I couldn't take care of her and to not call or text his phone again and hung up in my face. This was his way of having control over the situation and manipulating me once again.

When Damon took Zina away from me and would not let me see her and talk to her, I almost lost it and wanted to give up. I felt helpless and alone. I was all by myself and didn't know what to do so I called the county police office and explained to them the situation and they stated that since he was her dad it was nothing they could do because we didn't have any court orders.

I could not believe that God was letting this happen to me. I did all that I could to be a good wife, become a good person and a good mother to all of our children. And all I wanted was some help. All I wanted was for him to help co-parent with me and not treat me like I was his enemy. I didn't think that was too much to ask from him because he was her father and we were still married.

He acted as if he hated my guts for ruining his life but he was the one who was cheating with multiple women. He was the one who had a baby. He was the one that could never come up no matter how hard I tried to help him. He was the one that had five cars repossessed during our marriage. And he was the one that left his family. Again, God spoke to me and said fear not my child vengeance is mine.

Since I was the only one in the apartment, I cried like I never have before. Yelling at God 'okay Lord you win! I surrender it all to you. No more fighting. No more trying to do things my way. No more trying to do things on my own.' and I felt this peace come over me and I knew that it was in God's hands now.

> ***"My spirit is broken, My days are extinguished, The grave is ready for me. Are not mockers with me? And does not my eye dwell on their provocation?"***
> ***Job 17:1-2 -NKJV***

A couple of days later, my friend called me and said that she had the urge to call and check up on me. I began to break down crying while telling her what happened between Damon and I. She began to pray over me and the situation. She also told me to inform my lawyer of what happened so that he could be aware of the situation and give me some advice on what to do.

I was feeling optimistic and very hopeful after the call with her and decided to send my lawyer a detail email about what transpired with Damon while it was still fresh on my mind. Again, that was such a freeing experience. . .

By the end of that week I felt like I needed to see my other friend and speak with her about the situation. She agreed to meet with me at a restaurant. I told her that I didn't have any money and she said don't worry about it and that dinner was on her. "We can go to Applebee's for the 2 for $20", and we both laughed. Which was good with me because I was hungry.

We met up around seven that night and as soon as we sat down she asked me what happened. I began telling her what happened between Damon and I the week before. When I was done, she tells me that she already knew that Damon was going to try and take Zina away from me because God showed her a couple of months before hand. Wait a minute, what?

I asked her why she didn't tell me, and she said that "she asked God what to do but He told her to do and say nothing." God wanted me to go through that situation to get my full attention. Well He had it then! "He said that he was breaking me further down, chipping away all of the things that was holding me back to develop me into the woman He needs me to be while trying to build up my character so that I can walk into the destiny he has for me." God wanted to know if He could trust me. And that was the realist thing that she has ever told me.

Seeking After God

While I began to wait, God was able to change me. Showed me things that I never knew, made me feel things that I've never felt. In order for you to get to the next level that God has for you he has to disrupt your life. Which is taking you through a process. It could be joyful, hurtful, peaceful, painful and a feeling of loneliness. But for me, He was stripping me of everything that I thought I had and everything that I thought I needed. God was breaking me from the need to be in control at all times. I did not fully understand what that meant, oh but did I learn really fast.

When I laid on my face before God and told Him that I submit it all to Him, everything that I have, everything that I am and every desire, He can have it. I was sorry for always doing things my way. I had to make the decision to repent from my soul all the mistakes that I made. Whether it was lying, stealing, cheating or having sex for all those years knowing that it was wrong and not Godly. I was tired of always being the problem solver. I was tired of always trying to figure it all out.

Who knew that saying Yes to God would come with all these challenges? God began to put me in uncomfortable situations that were rough and ugly, but He was humbling me so that I could become the best servant that He wanted me to be. He told me to be still. But fear crept in because I wasn't able to pay all of my bills. "There is no fear in love, but perfect love cast out fear." I love God but I still tried to do things on my own. I figured that if I did small stuff it would be okay. I started doing uber eats delivering food. That was really helpful for me being able to grind it out since I didn't have Zina. I was making $200 - $300 every week.

I was able to have gas money. I was able to buy food and household products again. I was so happy because I was able to buy my daughter some new school shoes. The ones she had before were too small and Damon wouldn't get her a new pair. I was doing that for a couple of months and I was tired but it was great to have money in my packet again. But that's not what God wanted me to do. Once again He told me to be still. Of course, I was like but why, He said, "Be still." I was like" but God, we have money now". This was the first time that I heard God and understood what He was saying to me the whole time.

He said 'Shaletha, I never told you to do those things in order to get money, you did. If you continue doing things off of your own strength, how will I get the Glory? I cried my butt off because that was the most practical thing God has ever told me.

After 30 days of meditation and being in isolation from my family and friends, I asked God could I get my baby back? This was the hardest situation that I have ever been in. All the things that I went through in my twenties couldn't compare to me not seeing or talking to my daughter. I couldn't eat, I wasn't sleeping. Honestly, I didn't know how I was going to work and function. Immediately after I got clear directions from God that I can take Zina back, I planned to go to his church on a Sunday because I knew that he would not make a seen there in front of everyone.

When that Sunday came, I could hardly contain myself. I got ready for church like normal, but my nerves wouldn't allow me to eat or drink anything. The entire time I was consulting God on the plan I had presented to Him just to make sure that it aligned up with His will. As I was driving to Damon's church, I prayed one last time that if Yahweh did not want me to go that route to let me know before I pulled into the parking lot.

Here was the moment of truth. I pulled into the church parking lot and parked my car, took a deep breath and went inside. Once I was inside the church it felt like I went into tunnel vision and I was only looking for

Zina. It seemed like I only had five minutes to get in and get out. And when I didn't see Zina I began to panic as if he knew that I was coming and had her hidden.

I finally saw my aunt and mouth to her where is Zina? She motioned to where she was sitting and I went to her and asked if she wanted to go with mommy? She was so happy to see me, but we didn't have time for that, I wanted to cry so bad from hearing her little voice, but I had to stay strong and focused on the task at hand. I asked her again did she want to go with me and she said yes, so I told her to get her things and let's go.

We made it back to my car and I was finally able to breath. All I could do was look at my little girl still holding back my tears, and I did not want to ruin the moment for her. I couldn't believe that I was having to do something like this with my husband, her father, a man of God so he claimed. All I knew this was not Godly, but it wasn't my battle to fight.

I had faith, but did I really have it in God? Was I really living a walk by faith life? Nope! At that point I had to openly and honestly surrender my life and my finances to God. It was rough but He was right there by my side. And when I tell you that for the next couple of months we did not want for anything, we did not need for anything. Who knew that giving up control and trusting in God I would have so much favor? I began to receive money in my account. We were offered groceries. And a couple of people helped me pay my car note so that I wouldn't be too far behind or get repossessed.

Praise and worship are all that I could do. I wouldn't leave the house most of the time because I would have prayer time at home just so that I could be in His presence. He wanted me to trust Him and not man. He wanted to protect me. He wanted my love and attention. He wanted to deepen my relationship with Him and no one else. He wanted to handle all my battles. And most importantly He wanted my heart for me to release control unto him.

I was able to attend church whenever I could. I was able to watch church online all day if I needed to. I was getting more into the word and praying more throughout the day. And I even began fasting more. This time really knowing and understanding what fasting meant to God.

I prayed to God that I would be able to make new friends and friends with kids around Zina's age. Because in my house she is an only child and she always wanted someone to come over. Not understanding that mommy didn't talk to those people anymore so it would be hard for me to make arrangements to get them. Every day when I picked her up from school, we would go to the park and she would play with the kids out there for a couple of hours and I would just sit and read.

I was seeking God in a way like I never have before. I wanted God to know that I was all in and that He could use me and trust me to do whatever assignment He wanted me to do. I was asking God to change me to be more like Him. I wanted Him to renew my mind so I kept my focus in the word and reading other Christian authors.

Months later God began to put me around Godly people and people who wanted the same things out of life as I did. To my surprise it was a lot of ladies that had kids around the same age as Zina and she loved it. We got along with all the new Christian people that God has placed in our lives so far so I can only imagine what was to come.

"I sought the Lord, and He heard me, And delivered me from all my fears. They looked to Him and were radiant, And their faces were not ashamed. This poor man cried out, and the Lord heard him, And saved him out of all his troubles. The angel of the Lord encamps all around those who fear Him, And delivers them."
Psalm 34:4-7 -NKJV

The Divorce

This divorce has been an emotional roller-coaster. Even though Damon had left us, I still did not know what he was thinking or what his motives were. He refused to speak to me about the situation and every time I tried to ask him questions he would get mad. I began to leave it alone. I wanted this insane situation to be over. I just wanted to be healed from all the hurt. I wanted to be whole so that I could move forward in my life.

Damon said that he would help me out with Zina but he never did. I did some research and found out that I could file abandonment on him but he had to be gone from the home for at least one year. And I also found out that you can put your spouse on child support if you are separated.

I called the attorney general's office to figure out what I needed to do because this was my first child, I had no previous knowledge of how this worked. I went online and completed all the information and waited for a phone call or a court date.

A month later I received a court date in the mail and was super nervous because I didn't know what to expect. But low and behold Damon didn't show up. They took me into the back office to explain the next steps and I was super mad because I had missed work and had to pay for parking.

Three months later I had another court date and sure enough Damon didn't show that time either. At this point I knew that he was trying to get over on the system. If he would help me like he said, I would have never filed for child support. I didn't want to put him on it anyways because he was already in the system for three kids and not paying so I knew that I wasn't going to get anything.

The clerk took me in the back again to inform me of the next steps. And I asked how is this going to work because I am the one taking off work to come down here, paying for parking and having to pay a sitter to sit with my child before school starts so that I can be at court on time. She stated at this time they would have to serve him at this point in order for him to show up at court.

I was explaining to my work mom what was going on and how the situation was stressing me out. She told me about free legal assistance and how they can help with your case if you qualify. I looked up the information and went to a location two days later to fill out an application.

After explaining my situation to a counselor on site he stated that he would submit my application for a lawyer because I definitely was going to need help with my case. That was nothing but God looking out for me once again because he knew what lied ahead.

Out of nowhere I received an email from Damon's lawyer stating that Damon had filed for divorce and that I needed to sign the paperwork. Believe it or not I didn't even get mad. I was actually jumping with joy on the inside thinking that this was finally going to come to an end so that I could move on with my life.

That was not the case here. Damon told his lawyer a bunch of lies I guess so that he could take his case. I ended up calling the lawyer to get an understanding of what was to happen next. He explained to me that I would need to sign the divorce waiver since Damon and I were in agreement of separating and get it notarized and email it back to him.

The next day I printed out the form and signed it. When I got off work, I went to my bank to get it notarized so that I could submit it to him as soon as possible. He told me that once he turned in all of the paperwork to the courts, we could be divorced within 30 days. I'm like okay, cool that will definitely work.

A week after that, I received a call from a law office stating that they have received my application and would be representing me in my case. This was nothing but God's favor, he knew that I would need help. Once I told him everything about my situation and that Damon's lawyer had me to sign forms for court, he was on top of everything.

The very next day he called me and asked me to come into the office so that I could sign paperwork stating that he would represent me and that I needed to sign a waiver because Damon's lawyer forgot to mention that the form I was signing was waving all my rights to the divorce and that they could go to court without me even knowing. He put a stop to that quick fast and in a hurry.

There was a lot of back and forth going because of what Damon told his lawyer. I didn't want to go through any of this, I didn't want to talk about his story/our story as to why we were no longer together. I just wanted what was fair and right for Zina and I. He didn't want to help me out with her, he didn't want to help me pay for her childcare or anything.

After Damon left, he said that he would do all these things for us since he is the one that left and I believed him. When it came time to state what I wanted out of the divorce I told them the main thing for me was getting some money back for the loan that I took out in my name for the down payment on the house. Which Damon said he would pay me back and I had the text messages to prove it.

Once again Damon's lawyer was completely shocked by what I told him. Then they came back with an audit that I had to provide him of all the things that I purchased within the marriage which was cool for me because I had all the receipts.

I submitted that information to the lawyer and two weeks later I received an email stating that Damon and I had talked and that if I don't drop the request for the money he would go after half of my 401k. I was like oh no devil you are a lie, you will not get any of my money that I worked hard for to take care of our family because you wanted to spend yours on going to hotels every week.

Once I told my lawyer that Damon lied and we did not talk or settle on an agreement, what would be the next step because I was not dropping my request for the money and he was not getting any of mine. In October 2017, the lawyer informed me he could submit a request for him to submit all of his documentation and receipts to see if it was something that we could use. Which Damon wouldn't have any!

At that time the lawyer was suggesting that I drop my claim for the money since Damon was going after my 401k. But that was something that I was not going to do. He didn't understand everything that I went through while being married to him. He didn't understand the hurt and pain that Damon put me through. He didn't understand all the emotional abuse that I went through for years.

I began talking with God about this situation because I wasn't asking for something out of the normal I just wanted what was fair to me. I wouldn't even be in this situation if Damon would have been honest. But no, he was the one who decided to live a double life cheating and keeping secrets about him having a baby with a girl that he met online.

It wasn't fair that he deceived me and the family. I would have never got a new house with him. I would have never got all those loans in my name. I could have used my credit and my money on a down payment to get a house for my daughter and I. Once I expressed my feelings to God and surrendered the situation to Him, a peace came over me.

Months went by and I didn't hear anything from my lawyer. But I wasn't worried because I knew that my Father had my back and no one else. I continued to pray and have my quiet time with the Lord. And then one night I received an email from my lawyer that he will not be representing me anymore and another lawyer in their office will take over my case. The crazy thing is I did not get mad or angry, I had this peace over me and I knew that I had to continue to trust and have faith in my Father that He was working everything out for my good.

It was around April 2018, and I haven't heard anything from the Attorney General's office or from the new lawyer. I gave them a call to check on the status of my cases. The lady that I spoke with at the child support office said that she didn't know why it was taking this long but since we both had lawyers it was tied into the divorce case and to check with my lawyer. So that is exactly what I did.

I called the law office so that I could get information on who my new contact person would be and surprisingly the lawyer answered the phone. She apologized for not calling me sooner and explained to me everything that was going on in the office. Therefore, we went over my case briefly just to get my side of the story and took some notes. She explained to me that she hasn't looked over all the documents that my previous lawyer left for her and that she will look over everything and give me a call within two weeks.

I was a little confused on what happened with the situation but I knew deep down that it only had to be God because I believe that the other lawyer was not doing his best on my behalf. We had sold the house the year before and we had only one child. I could not understand why it was taking this long to get a court date. Two weeks into May the lawyer called me to inform me that she looked over everything and needed to ask me some questions about the case.

For some reason she did not understand why Damon had not been served yet and that was definitely news to me. I told her that I wasn't sure on why that was when our lawyers had been in communication with each other this whole time. She immediately put a plan into action so that we could get the ball rolling for a court date.

On June the 11th she called me and said that she had spoken to Damon and he agreed to sign a waiver for him not to be served and that he would come to court. We had a court date set for June 13th at 8 o'clock am. 'Look at God, Won't He do it?!' I knew right then that was nothing but God working on my behalf. Since He did that for me, I told my Father that I would drop my request for Damon to pay me back the money. I had to have total trust in Him. I had to have complete faith that He was going to supply all of my needs.

It was summer time and Zina was out of school and I could not find anyone to keep her and I couldn't afford to place her in a summer program. I emailed the lawyer to inform her of my situation and she told me to bring her anyway but the judge does not allow kids in the courtroom. I said okay because I had no other choice.

I was feeling really positive the day of court. I arrived 30 minutes early because I didn't want to be late; then minor things started to happen. I ended up sitting at the wrong courtroom for 30 minutes. I didn't have the lawyer's cell number and couldn't call her. Then I thought about sending her an email to let her know that I was there on time and did not know where the courtroom was and to call me on my cell phone.

Minutes went by and nothing. I was freaking out because I did not want to miss court and have to reschedule because I already had taken off work for that day. Fifteen minutes later the lawyer called and directed me to where she was and what she had on so that I could find her. Zina and I took off down the hallway looking for her and we finally made it. She informed me that Damon was there with his lawyer. Thankfully, the Judge was not mad. She talked to us about Zina being in there and said that she could sit in her office until court was over. I was so grateful for that. I did not want her to sit outside the courtroom by herself.

The judge was asking Zina all types of questions and commenting her on how pretty she was. She even offered Zina some candy and water. The bailiff took Zina to the back and court began. I asked my lawyer did she have all the documents that the previous lawyer had for my case and she told me that he only left the documents that Damon's lawyer submitted to him back in November 2017. I felt my blood rising because she could have told me that beforehand and I could have brought all my documents. I took a deep breath because worrying wasn't going to help anything now and silently prayed to God.

> "Lord you said that vengeance is yours, you said that you were going to fight my battles, you said that I am your daughter and you take care of your children, Father I only want what's fair for my daughter and I."

Then the judge called me up first. I was super nervous and didn't know what to expect because I was not aware that we would be talking. She began asking me why I have Zina with me and I explained to her that I didn't have any help and that Damon hasn't seen her since March of that year and when school was out I reached out to him to help me with Zina for the summer and he did not reply back.

The judge was upset about what I was telling her. She couldn't believe that he was treating her like that. She asked me all types of things about our relationship, our marriage and why we are not together anymore. I did not want to talk about this but I stayed strong so that I wouldn't get emotional. She asked me about our debt; my debt. I told the truth about everything and then the million-dollar question was asked, "Where are your documents?" I was hot because my previous lawyer had everything. Everything that was in my name, everything that was in both of our names. The loans that I had taken out in my name and the copies of the checks that showed me giving Damon the down payment money for the house.

The lawyer did explain to the judge how she just took over this case and did not have proper time to go over everything. It was Damon's turn to go up to the judge and she began asking him questions and asked him why he haven't seen his daughter since March 2018, and typical, Damon lied. He was lying about everything and had gotten mad that I brought up his other baby. I didn't understand why he still was not claiming that child when he knew that it was his son; he's been keeping him since we were not together anymore.

The judge asked him if he had any documentation that he wanted to present to her and of course they didn't have any. Since they requested that Damon should get half of my 401k the judge denied the request and was not having it. She was already upset with him for leaving his family and not taking care of his child. She asked him what makes him entitled to get some of my money when he is the one that left, he had no answer for her. Since I couldn't provide her with my documents she stated that I would leave with what I came with and he would leave with what he came with and granted us the divorce.

I almost jumped out of my skin with excitement "hallelujah, thank you Jesus" because I heard stories of people having to go back to court or the judge telling the couple to try and work it out and then come back. But that was not the case here because I knew that the Lord was my judge. She went over our rules, dates and time for him to see Zina and then the child support money and medical care. I guess that Damon was caught up in his feelings about not getting any of my 401k that he did not pay attention to the amount that was awarded to me.

When I tell you that daddy showed out for me, He really did. I am so glad that I listened and obeyed Abba because the money that was awarded to me was the same amount that I was initially asking Damon to pay me back. (praise break!) I didn't hear anything else after that. They said that it would take about 30 days for everything to be signed by the appropriate people and put into the system then we will be officially divorced. I left that day feeling awesome, feeling free and feeling like I accomplished something.

Days, weeks, months went by and I didn't hear from my lawyer. I was beginning to get nervous about them catching the monthly child support and wondered if the amount was going to change. And God reminded me that He got this, everything is working out for my good. At this point it was nothing else for me to do but give my all to God. What was I going to lose? In my mind I had already lost everything. And this is the one thing that I had not done before. I made a commitment to God and myself that I would do a 21-day fast in August 2018.

"Father, teach me how to walk in a manner that is pleasing to you. I long for a closer relationship with you. And I know that praying and fasting is the only way that I can truly humbly submit myself to you, in order for you to release everything that you have in store for me."

I can't believe that two days later after I prayed that prayer, my lawyer called to tell me that my divorce was final. Words could not express the feeling that I was feeling. No more back and forth with Damon. No more worrying about him lying on me. No more missing work going to court for him not to show up. And more importantly, no more of him stating that he wasn't going to see his daughter until the divorce is final.

"Furthermore it has been said, Whoever divorces his wife, let him give her a certificate of divorce." Matthew 5:31 -NKJV

Now that we have a court order which is an official proclamation from the judge, there are rules set into place for both of us and if he doesn't follow them he would be held accountable for his actions by the courts and by his Heavenly Father.

> *"Rejoice always, pray without ceasing, in everything give thanks; for this is the will of God in Christ Jesus for you."*
>
> **1 Thessalonians 5:16-8 -NKJV**

"Father, thank you for using my pain to transform me to look more like you. And for using it to free me from control and fear that the enemy tried to place over my life. You said that no weapon formed against me shall prosper. Thank you for the blessings that you have over my life. Thank you for reminding me that I am a child of the Most High and that the battle is not mine but yours. In Jesus name, Amen!"

As I look back over my life, there were plenty of times that God was trying to get my attention. If I would have submitted my life over to Him sooner, I wouldn't have gotten off the railroad track that was already laid for me. If I would have just listened that first time my Father spoke to me I would be walking in my purpose, not God having to reroute my tracks that were already set into motion.

But through it all I do not regret anything that has happened in my past, because I know no matter how long it takes, Abba Father will eventually get you there. I am the daughter of the Most High and that I am a Queen and deserve to have a King that is after God's own heart and walking in His purpose. I don't have to change a man. I don't have to build a man up and help him figure out his identity. I will have the Kingdom life that God has intended me to live while walking in my spiritual purpose. I am leaving my past in the rearview mirror and looking forward into my future.

> *"Brethren, I do not regard myself as having laid hold of it yet; but one thing I do: forgetting what lies behind and reaching forward to what lies ahead, I press on toward the goal for the prize of the upward call of God in Christ Jesus. Let us therefore, as many as are perfect, have this attitude; and if in anything you have a different attitude, God will reveal that also to you"*
>
> **Philippians 3:13-15 NASB**

I am truly happy for God's grace and mercy over my life. I could have died a long time ago but He spared my life for a reason and I will forever be grateful that He did because I have a wonderful six-year-old daughter that I can be the example for. Today I understand what the saying "God is a good God" means. I know that he is a sovereign God that has a great future in store for me and my little one. And He has a great future in store for you, so learn to let go and love yourself and allow God to give you His love. I pray that you too will seek God for understanding of the plan that He has for your life. And allow God to heal you from the inside out so that you can become a light for someone else. Remember to be patient and wait on the Lord. The key to God's heart is obedience and submission.

Love you all and hope that my story was a blessing to you!

> *"Which He will bring about at the proper time - He who is the blessed and only Sovereign, the King of kings and Lord of lords."*
>
> **1 Timothy 6:15 -NASB**

ABOUT THE AUTHOR

Shaletha Marshall was born and raised in Dallas, Texas from a suburban area. She is the mother of daughter Zion Marshall. She has many years of being a trainer and leader at whatever she does. Shaletha founded Creative Link Coaching that is dedicated to helping divorce women find their paths in life. She will continue to help women discover their personal and professional goals. She offers emotional support and daily motivation for developing your confidence and clarity that's needed to have a successful kingdom, Godly life.

www.creativelinkcoaching.com

www.ingramcontent.com/pod-product-compliance
Lightning Source LLC
Chambersburg PA
CBHW031350160426

43196CB00007B/797